INVASION OF PRIVACY AND THE LAW

28 Cornerstone Court Decisions Every Officer and PI Should Know

RON HANKIN

43-08 162nd Street
Flushing, NY 11358
www.LooseleafLaw.com
800-647-5547

This publication is not intended to replace nor be a substitute for any official procedural material issued by your agency of employment nor other official source. Looseleaf Law Publications, Inc., the author and any associated advisors have made all possible efforts to ensure the accuracy and thoroughness of the information provided herein but accept no liability whatsoever for injury, legal action or other adverse results following the application or adoption of the information contained in this book.

©2013 Looseleaf Law Publications, Inc. All rights reserved. No part of this book may be reproduced, stored in a retrieval system, or transcribed, in any form or by any means, electronic, mechanical, photocopying, recording, or otherwise, without the prior written permission of the Copyright owner. For such permission, contact Looseleaf Law Publications, Inc., 43-08 162nd Street, Flushing, NY 11358, (800) 647-5547, www.LooseleafLaw.com.

Hankin, Ronald M.
  Invasion of privacy & the law : 28 cornerstone court decisions every officer & P.I. should know / Ron Hankin.
      pages cm
  Includes index.
  ISBN 978-1-60885-059-4
  1. Privacy, Right of--United States--Cases. 2. Criminal investigations--United States--Cases. 3. Police--United States--Cases. 4. Police, Private--Legal status, laws, etc.--United States--Cases. 5. Private investigators--Legal status, laws, etc.--United States--Cases. I. Title.
  KF1262.H36 2013
  342.7308'58--dc23
                                                                2013018999

> It is only for ease of reading that the masculine pronoun is predominantly used herein. No slight was intended toward women PIs or law enforcement officers.

> Cover by *Sans Serif,* Saline, Michigan

Table of Contents

Author's Note i

About the Author iii

Introduction v

Part One: Private Detectives 1
  Chapter One INVASION OF PRIVACY 1
    The Tort: Four Branches of Invasion of Privacy 1
  Chapter Two SURVEILLANCE AND RELATED ISSUES 5
    Case 1 – *Forster v. Manchester* (Pa., 1963) 5
    2A: Intrusive Surveillance 11
    Rules of Safe Surveillance 13
      Case 2 – *Souder v. Pendleton* (La., 1956) 14
    2B: Stalking 17
    2C: Lawful Purpose 18
      Case 3 – *Nastal v. Henderson* (Mich., 2006) 18
    2D: Ruse 21
      Case 4 – *Furman v. Sheppard* (Md., 1998) 23
      Case 5 – *Burns v. Musterbrand Cabinets* (Il., 2007) 26
      Case 6 – *Noble v. Sears* (Calif., 1973) 28
    2E: Trespass 30
      Case 7 – *McCain v. Boise Cascade* (Or., 1975) 31
    2F: Invasive Trespass 34
      Case 8 – *Miller v. Brooks* (NC, 1996) 34
  Chapter Three PROCURING AND SELLING CONFIDENTIAL
    INFORMATION 37
      Case 9 – *Keyzer v. Amerlink* (NC, 2005) 37
    3A: Credit Information 40
      Case 10 – *Phillips v. Grendahl* (8th Cir., 2002) 41
    3B: Sale of Unpublished Information 45
      Case 11 – *Remsburg v. Docusearch* (N.H., 2003) 45
  Chapter Four DISCLOSING PRIVATE FACTS 53
    Case 12 – *Johnson v. K-mart* (Ill., 2002) 53
  Chapter Five FALSE LIGHT 57
    Case 13 – *Association Services, Inc. v. Smith*
      (Ga., 2001) 57

Part Two: Police 61
  Chapter Six THE REASONABLE EXPECTATION OF PRIVACY 61
    6A: Warrant, Exceptions, and Non-Search 62
  Chapter Seven PRIVATE SECURITY 65

Case 14 – *Gillett v. Texas* (Tx., 1979) 65
Case 15 – *State v. Buswell* (Minn., 1990) 67
Chapter Eight BODY SEARCH 71
Case 16 – *Hidey v. Ohio State Highway Patrol*
(Ohio, 1996) 71
Chapter Nine SCHOOL SEARCHES 75
Case 17 – *Thomas v. Roberts* (11th Cir., 2001) 75
Chapter Ten SCOPES AND THE NATURAL EYE, ETC. 81
Case 18 – *State v. Jones* (Wash., 1982) 84
Case 19 – *State v. Louis* (Or., 1983) 85
Case 20 – *People v. Arno* (Cal., 1979) 87
Chapter Eleven NON-ELECTRONIC EAVESDROP 91
Case 21 – *U.S. v. Mankani* (2nd Cir, 1984) 91
Chapter Twelve PRIVATE SPACE 95
12A: Privacy Stalls 95
Case 22 – *Liebman v. State* (Texas, 1983) 95
Case 23 – *Green v. State* (Tex., 1978) 100
Case 24 – *People v. Mercado* (NY, 1986) 102
12B: Changing Rooms 105
Case 25 – *Trujillo v. City of Ontario* (Cal., 1996) 105
Case 26 – *Bevans v. Smartt* (D. Utah, 2004) 108
Chapter Thirteen ABANDONED PROPERTY 115
Case 27 – *U.S. v. Hernandez* (10th Cir.,1993) 115
Chapter Fourteen TRASH 119
Case 28 – *U.S. v. Hendricks* (7th Cir., 1991) 119

Table of Cases 123

Index 125

Author's Note

For an investigator who surreptitiously watches an individual without court authority, there is always the risk of invasion of privacy. Not only watching, but also listening without a warrant or approved warrant exception may well bring any investigator, whether private or governmental, to the brink of criminal and civil sanctions. For the field operative who does not have legal advice close at hand, snap decisions easily can result in the operative stepping over the fine line which separates an aggressive lawful observation from an illegal intrusion.

This book, *Invasion of Privacy and the Law*, attempts to provide some answers to the investigator's quandary of what is right and what is wrong when approaching individual privacy. It provides answers in the same way most lawyers would resolve any such dilemma—by using legal precedent as a guide. Included in these pages are twenty-eight privacy court cases, selected as a mix of those in which the investigator has acted properly with some in which the actions were deemed illegal.

By way of factual illustrations and the court's own words, the book discusses investigative conduct deemed acceptable or that deemed actionable. The factual scenarios created are, at times, exaggerated to make easier an understanding of the issues which faced the investigator; followed by the court's actual words approving or condemning the investigator's actions.

About the Author

Ron Hankin earned his bachelor's degree from the Medill School of Journalism, Northwestern University, and his Juris Doctor from Chicago's IIT Kent College of Law. He served the U.S. Marine Corps as rifle company commander and Commanding Officer for Security for the Navy Prison, San Diego, California. He left the Corps a major. He then served the FBI under J. Edgar Hoover as Special Agent working criminal investigations and fugitive apprehension, before entering the private practice of law.

After a career in the law, Ron operated a private detective agency specializing in domestic surveillance. He has a commercial pilot's license. As owner-pilot of over twenty aircraft during his flying career, Ron has participated in numerous air-shows throughout the Midwest in his authentically restored Marine Corps SNJ Texan, Twin Beech, and AT-19.

Currently he owns and operates Accurate Investigation, Ltd. and lives in a suburb northwest of Chicago with wife Camille and their mutts, Daisy Mae and Daisy Deuce. His son Craig lives nearby with wife Patti and three grandchildren, MacKenzie, Kylie, and Addison.

Introduction

The right to privacy is not mentioned in the U.S. Constitution. The right arises from federal and state court interpretations of the document's Fourth Amendment prohibition against unreasonable governmental search and seizure. Those interpretations continually expand the protections provided individual privacy; hence, a government investigator must always presume that any warrantless surreptitious view or overhear may draw Fourth Amendment attention. As for the Private Investigator (PI), though not generally bound by the Fourth Amendment, individual privacy is a foremost concern. He (or she) operates in an occupational world steeped in privacy protections. A single overstep can easily result in successful suit or criminal sanction against him for invasion of privacy brought by his subject or some innocent third person.

No short book could possibly cover every possible scenario an investigator faces in his work day in terms of privacy invasion. While the heavy concentration of cases obviously involves watching and listening, privacy invasion is broader than that, including such acts as release of personal information. What we have attempted in *Invasion of Privacy and the Law* is to highlight general rules of avoidance gleaned from the study of milestone cases. Make no mistake: There are few safe harbors in spying without warrant. We are helped, however, by those who have gone before us. Included here are twenty-eight such investigators, persons, who, operating without warrant, stumbled into a factual situation so unique at the time it is used today as court precedent.

Our court decisions involving privacy, including the parameter of warrantless searches, usually start with a reference to the 1967 case of *Katz v. United States*, the cornerstone of privacy protection; so shall we.

Katz v. United States (389 U.S. 347, 1967)

Defendant Katz shut the door to a public phone booth and used the phone to transmit illegal gaming wagers interstate. He was under FBI surveillance at the time and agents attached a recording device to the exterior of the phone booth, recording the conversation. He was convicted and on appeal to the Court of Appeals, his conviction was affirmed. The court noted Katz was in plain view of the public while in the booth and that there had been no governmental physical intrusion into the phone booth itself. However, on appeal to the U.S. Supreme Court, the case was accepted for review. Ultimately, the Court reversed, overturning his conviction. In concluding that an expectation of privacy, not the physical location in which he stood, made the governmental action illegal, the Court said:

"The government's activities ...violated the privacy upon which (Katz) justifiably relied while using the telephone booth and thus constituted a 'search and seizure" within the meaning of the Fourth Amendment...One who occupies (a telephone booth), shuts the door behind him, and pays the toll that permits him to place a call is surely entitled to assume that the words he utters into the microphone will not be broadcast to the world...."

While the facts of *Katz* did not specifically discuss photographs, video, or the use of scopes, the case redefined the meaning of Fourth Amendment search and seizure. No longer was legality of a search based on the place that an observation was made as much as whether the person observed had a reasonable expectation in the privacy in what he was doing. Most investigators, whether student of constitutional law or not, now know that any person who is surreptitiously watched or listened to, under carefully delineated circumstances, has a shield of privacy protection for any action he has reason to believe is private—even, under some circumstances, as in *Katz*, the action is illegal. Should the expectation of privacy be shown reasonable, a warrant or warrant exception is necessary to observe the action (warrant exceptions are numerous, vary by jurisdiction, and are discussed in much greater detail in *Navigating the Legal Minefields of Private Investigations*, Ron Hankin, *Looseleaf Law Publications, Inc.,* 2008).

Note that the Fourth Amendment prohibition against unlawful search and seizure is applicable only to arms of the government and on face does not apply to private investigators

(PI's) and private security personnel unless they are operating in concert with government agents. We quickly note, however, that both the PI and security officer do not operate without privacy restraints. Far from it. The tort of invasion of privacy provides severe sanctions for privacy "intrusions outrageous to the reasonable person." This tort closely mirrors the ideology of *Katz* and its "reasonable expectation of privacy." In general, the courts have used the terms interchangeably. What all this means is that an observation procured by a government agent with intent to use same as evidence in a court of law must be procured with a warrant, or warrant exception, or taken under circumstances in which his subject has no reasonable expectation of privacy—a non-search. So, too, the private investigator should realize that any observation he makes which will see the light of day must be procured in a manner that satisfies the reasonable privacy expectations of the so-called "reasonable person."

Of great help to any investigator is a basic legal tenet that an act done in public generally negates a claim of a reasonable expectation of privacy. Remember, *Katz* was an aural intrusion of a private conversation, not a visual observation. In general a visual observation or photographic image taken of the subject or his actions while he is in the public-way is a classic example of an instance where the subject has no reasonable expectation of privacy. This principle is the foundation of search and seizure as well as non-governmental privacy cases.

Said the Court in Katz:

{W}hat a person knowingly exposes to the public, even in his own home or office, is not a subject of Fourth Amendment protection...."
But the statement is far from a safe harbor, as the case demonstrates, when the Court goes on to state: " ...(B)ut what he seeks to preserve as private, even in an area accessible to the public may be constitutionally protected...."

The purpose here is to provide specific precedent cases that help clarify the dichotomy of *Katz*. To wit: that not all that is public is privacy unprotected; and not all that is private is privacy protected. The point of *Katz* is that the subject's claim of privacy is based on his reasonable expectation, not necessarily the physical location from which the observation, whether visual or aural, is made. So we see that an observation or photograph taken from a place in which any other third persons with lawful access could have taken the same view—had they chosen to do so—may diminish or even negate a claim of a reasonable expectation of privacy.

While the facts of our 28 cases are somewhat exaggerated to better define the issue involved, the actual opinion of the real world court is verbatim. These cases have been selected because they are commonly cited by courts which rely on legal precedent to assist in applying *Katz*. While the facts of any given case may differ, invariably a court will rely on what has gone before and will use cases like those included here as a good starting point. So, too, these cases are for us a good starting point.

PART ONE: PRIVATE DETECTIVES

Chapter One
INVASION OF PRIVACY

Tort remedies provide financial redress to an individual whose privacy has been invaded. This remedy is a cause of action separate from other relief available for the same act, such as trespass, defamation, and the like. Invasion of privacy stands on its own as a threat to any PI or police officer even when free of other infractions.

For those interested in the genesis of this protection, it is fairly current as law theories go. A 1960 law review article by a respected law school dean, William L. Prosser, suggested privacy rights were ripe for development. Prosser had great influence on those who shaped our common law—federal and state judges. Prosser's theory espoused that privacy actually consisted of four separate intrusions, all variations of an individual's "right to be let alone."

Each of the four intrusions—called "branches"—is accepted in varying degrees by every jurisdiction. A review of the four branches provides valuable insight into what is acceptable conduct by a private investigator or police officer and that which is not.

The Tort: Four Branches of Invasion of Privacy

1. Intrusion of Solitude and Seclusion – physical or electronic intrusion into one's private space.

This tort is of paramount concern to a private investigator—intrusion is at the heart of his workday. In fact, he skates at the edges anytime he probes someone's private affairs. The tort consists of four elements: (1) an intentional and substantial intrusion (physical or electronic) occurs into the solitude or seclusion of the claimant; (2) the intrusion is highly offensive to the reasonable person; (3) the matter intruded into is private; that is, the claimant had a reasonable expectation of privacy in the subject matter; and (4) the intrusion has caused anguish and suffering for which he should be compensated. Make no mistake: It doesn't take much to open the cash register. A single peep into someone's bedroom window may satisfy all four elements.

It is the second element that is the center of our attention: the act offensive to the "reasonable person." Who is this reasonable person? Rather than seeking him out, one might find it easier to study the conduct that offends him. Precedent cases provide a sufficient heads-up that any PI or police officer perusing the material in this book will get a head start into conduct that works or which is to be avoided.

2. Public Disclosure of Private Facts – dissemination to third persons of private information that embarrasses the claimant, even when the information is true.

The crux of the tort of public disclosure is release of private facts of the victim to persons who have no need to know such information. The four elements of the tort: (1) disclosure to the public (2) of a private fact (3) highly offensive in the eyes of a reasonable person that (4) the recipient has no legitimate need to know.

Truth is not available as a defense to a private detective who communicates irrelevant private information to his client. Cases consistently hold that the "public" aspect is satisfied by disclosure of the information to a small group of persons who have special relationship to the claimant, such as fellow church members, co-employees, work supervisors, or family members.

3. False Light – publication of information that places a person in a false light, even though the information is not defamatory.

Elements of the tort include: (1) information is communicated highly offensive to a reasonable person, and (2) the defendant knew or acted in reckless disregard of the embarrassment it would cause. False light differs from defamation in that false light does not require the communication be false.

The crux of false light is that misleading information has been published of extreme embarrassment to the claimant. In some instances, both defamation and false light are available for the same communication. One advantage to the victim of false light, unlike defamation, is that actual damages need not be shown. In some jurisdictions, false light is the cause of action of choice for an allegation of illegal or immoral conduct when there is misidentification. A PI should always make every effort to identify his subject by photograph and limit confidential reports to the client.

4. Appropriation – the unauthorized use of a person's name or likeness to obtain some benefit.

The tort consists of three elements: (1) appropriation, (2) of another's name or likeness with "intrinsic value," (3) for the use or benefit of another. The crux is not the use, but the benefit. This branch differs from the other three in that injury is not based on hurt feelings, sensibilities, or offensive actions, but rather, the value of the use. A PI using another person's identity to benefit himself in some way, such as access to a closed event, might face a claim under this tort.

Chapter Two
SURVEILLANCE AND RELATED ISSUES

For many private detectives, their first concern in watching someone do a private act is personal safety. By nature of the work, the PI interacts with persons who are under tremendous stress—perhaps involved in marital infidelity or the commission of crime. An experienced PI knows that a cornered marital cheat can be every bit as dangerous as someone caught stealing from a loading dock at midnight. Facing personal danger when tailing a stressed-out target is bad, but the risks do not end there. Perhaps more insidious, yes, but the PI faces another very grave danger: this to his personal estate by way of claim for invasion of privacy. Then it is his pocket book under siege.

The duty of the private investigator to ascertain the truth, veracity, and location of persons is not taken lightly by courts; accordingly, any person with something to hide should assume he is under PI scrutiny. As the following cases demonstrate, courts appreciate not only the strategic role played by the private investigator in the scheme of things, but also the fine line he must walk to avoid intrusion into privacy. But when he crosses the line, courts show him little mercy. Perhaps, the most perplexing real time decision the private investigator makes on a daily basis is when to stop the surveillance. That is, when does an aggressive surveillance turn into harassment?

Case 1
Forster v. Manchester (Pa., 1963)

Claims manager Keyes studied the claim on his desk. Thirty years of claim work had not instilled patience in Keyes and whenever a claimant's attorney called him on the telephone the day after an accident pushing for settlement, his competitive juices flowed. In this case, the call was from Sy Sly, a well-known injury attorney. Sly gave Keyes a bottle of bourbon every Christmas and

Keyes gladly took it and drank it. But Sly's name came up on too many bogus claims for Keyes to ever cut him some slack.

   The facts known to Keyes to that point showed Sly's client was stopped at a red light when her car was lightly tapped from the rear. The damage, if any, was minimal and the claimant made no mention of injury at the time. When Sly called, however, he said his client, Ms. Bumpkin, was under doctor's care for serious traumatic injuries to neck and back; and Sly wanted to know if Keyes wanted to talk quick settlement to save the insurance company a lot of expense. Keyes thanked Sly for his deep and sincere concern for the insurance company but said he would wait to settle on another day. Keyes next call was to Private Detective Jack Heart with instructions to investigate Ms. Bumpkin's injuries.

   Heart drove to Bumpkin's home to start surveillance but a quick perusal of the property told him videotaping her activities around the house would be difficult. The house had privacy fencing on all sides of the property. His surveillance would be confined to the public way. Unfortunately, unless Bumpkin ventured out of the house, a determination of the extent of Bumpkin's injuries would be in the hands of doctors working for Sy Sly.

   Heart need not have worried. The garage door soon went up and Bumpkin drove off in her Buick. She drove to a local store. When she exited her car, Heart noted Bumpkins wore a neck brace and walked with apparent difficulty. Heart knew a neck brace and limp come with the territory when investigating fraudulent claims. He assumed Attorney Sly had briefed his client that she might be watched.

   On day two, Bumpkin went to the store again, and once again wore the brace and limped. The third day,

Chapter Two

Heart was joined by another PI that Keyes sent out. It was typical Keyes's impatience. He sent Ace Cannon, an aggressive go-getter, to help the laid-back but more experienced Heart in hopes of getting the better of Sy Sly and Bumpkin. Investigative money was not a problem with Keyes if he smelled a bogus claim. To upend fraud, Keyes would spend whatever was necessary; on the other hand, he demanded results and demanded them fast. Cannon would, therefore, join Heart. On the whole, the two were a totally typical PI team.

Sitting in Heart's van that third day, the investigators watched as Bumpkin's garage door came up and the Buick backed out. Probably going to the store, as usual, Heart figured. They followed the Buick to a local store, where Bumpkin exited the vehicle wearing the neck brace and walking with an exaggerated limp. But this time Heart sensed she knew she was being watched. A PI develops a sense for when his target is also watching him.

On the ride home, traffic forced Heart's van alongside Bumpkin's Buick at a stop light—a woeful misadventure for any hardworking PI. "Don't make eye contact," Heart said calmly, staring straight ahead. But the warning was too late for the overly aggressive Cannon, who already had his camera up making a gratuitous video of Bumpkin staring back at him. The Buick peeled rubber at the light change with Cannon pounding the van's dash. "Let's go, man, you'll lose her!"

"We're done for today," was all Heart said. He made the next turn and headed for his office. It was a rule of Heart's that if there ever was any question of a burned surveillance, he'd let things cool. It is a fine line between harassment and aggressive surveillance. Heart waited two days before he and Cannon were back on the case. Once again Bumpkin's Buick drove off with Heart in pursuit. Alas, this time they got no further than the street corner when the Buick abruptly stopped. There Bumpkin rolled down her window apparently waiting for them to pull alongside; but Heart drove by her and again terminated the surveillance.

That afternoon, Keyes received a telephone call from Attorney Sy Sly. "Your people are following my client," he said, "and I want it stopped! That is harassment!"

"I don't know what you're talking about, Sy," Keyes said. "I have no surveillance going of your client. If I did, counsel, you should know that I would be duty bound to tell you. We'll just leave it to the doctors to decide how badly she's hurt; that okay, Sly?" Sy Sly agreed that would be best.

The next day Heart brought in a new vehicle, this one rented, and again he and Cannon picked up Bumpkin's trail. But this time, for a change of pace, they picked up the Buick at the exit to Bumpkin's subdivision and were lucky enough to keep their distance while she drove cross town. They were pleasantly perplexed when she drove to a tennis club, parked and walked from the car to the building without either the neck brace or limp, and carrying a tennis racquet.

Heart heard about Keyes's conversation with the claimant's attorney and guessed that Sy Sly had told Bumpkin the heat was off, and that he had backed the insurance company down when he told them to stay away. Or Sy might have believed Keyes was honest when he said they were not following Bumpkin. In any event, Heart had seen it before. He told the younger Cannon that it was his experience most claimants out to scam an insurance company are creatures of habit; given enough time, they will prematurely return to what for them are normal activities. They like the idea of making money on a claim, but don't like the inconvenience of having to forego life's pleasures, like golf, yard work, or, in this case, tennis.

Inside the tennis facility, Heart watched Bumpkin play a few sets of team tennis, which he captured on hidden video. When Heart's subsequent report was provided to attorney Sly with Keyes's denial of the claim, the attorney was back on the phone to Keyes. "Keyes, I'm going to sue you, your company, and your gumshoes for invasion of privacy. One, they continued to follow my client after she discovered them—that is harassment—and two, you denied the surveillance when I specifically confronted you about it. That is unethical and illegal. You disappoint me, Keyes."

"Counsel," Keyes said, lighting a cigar, "I have no more legal obligation to explain the actions of my PIs in the course of their duties than police have in explaining the next move of their detectives."

"But you lied to me."

"Sy, there's good lies and there's bad lies. About time you learned the difference."

Sy Sly filed suit against the insurance company and the investigators on behalf of his client, claiming ethical and privacy violations, harassment, and stalking.

In a 1963 case with similar facts, though in its day film, not video, was the mode of picture-taking, the Supreme Court of Pennsylvania discussed two common privacy issues confronting a private investigator such as Heart in following a claimant. Specifically, (1) is it privacy invasion for a private investigator to continue the surveillance after his presence is discovered? and (2) is it actionable, when confronted, to deny the investigatory surveillance?

In siding with the investigators, the court in *Forster v. Manchester* discussed the importance and necessity of surveillance by private detectives in performance of their duties.

Said the court:

In determining the extent of the interest to be protected, we must take cognizance of the fact that [the insurance claimant/appellant] has made a claim for personal injuries ... It is not uncommon for defendants in accident cases to employ investigators to check on the validity of claims against them. Thus, by making a claim for personal injuries appellant must expect reasonable inquiry and investigation to be made of her claim and to this extent her interest in privacy is circumscribed. It should also be noted that all of the surveillances took place in the open on public thoroughfares where appellant's activities could be observed by passers-by. To this extent [she] exposed herself to public observation and therefore is not entitled to the same degree of privacy that she would enjoy within the confines of her own home.

*Moving to the question of whether [the investigator/appellee's] conduct is reasonable, we feel that there is much social utility to be gained from these investigations. It is in the best interests of society that valid claims be ascertained and fabricated claims be exposed. The legislature recognized the importance of these investigative activities in the Private Detective Act of 1953 when it defined the business of a licensed private detective to include investigations of the 'identity, habits, conduct, movements, whereabouts * * * of any person' and, in another subsection when it authorized the 'securing of evidence to be used * * * in the trial of civil * * * cases.' Certainly, following the subject during her daily activities and recording on film her movements and whereabouts is consonant with the wording of the Act and the aforementioned social purpose.*

There was nothing unreasonable in the manner in which [she] was followed nor in the taking of motion pictures. In regard to the surveillance, it was conducted by experienced investigators who did not use improper techniques. [The investigator] testified that he tried to stay at least a block behind appellant in his automobile. The few times ... [he] was observed by appellant were not intentional but purely inadvertent. During the course of an extended automobile surveillance in heavy traffic, it is not an unreasonable occurrence for an investigator's vehicle to pass close by the vehicle he is following. In fact, it was in the investigator's best interests to remain as unobtrusive as possible because if the subject were aware of his presence she would not behave in a natural manner. Moreover, there was no trespassing on appellant's property nor spying through her windows as is present in the cases cited by appellant.

Counsel for appellant maintains that the defense of social utility is not available to appellee since the insurance company's out-of-court denial of responsibility served as a waiver which binds appellee. We do not agree. In order for a detective to carry out successfully an assignment it is essential that the identity of his client remain secret ... Hence, it would have frustrated the purpose of the investigation for [the insurance company] to admit that it was responsible for the surveillance ... We therefore hold that the facts and circumstances as herein described do not establish that appellant's right to privacy has been invaded.

Forster v. Manchester, 189 A2d 147 (Pa 1963)

2A: Intrusive Surveillance

A private detective might chalk up a "burned" surveillance to bad luck; but usually luck has nothing to do with it. Until he finds a way to go invisible, a PI cannot ride tail or park in the street outside a house for extended periods and not expect to be seen.

Often the reason the gumshoe stays longer on that day's surveillance than he should is cost: it is expensive to break off a surveillance not knowing if funds exist to pick it up again later. Most PIs do not have a deep-pocket insurance company funding their surveillance activities. Most individual clients balk at the expense of calling off surveillance just because the investigator suspects he's been spotted. There is cost to go out and back again;

there is also the sixty-four dollar question whether he will even catch up with the subject again; or whether the operative and car should be changed. Hence the hapless gumshoe, caught in a trick bag, pushes the envelope trying to do in one trip what should take two or three.

At some point he is discovered but he soldiers on anyway. When bad things follow, this is not bad luck. The fact is most operations cannot be completed in a single surveillance, or even two, so good judgment must trump impatience. It is the rare occasion an investigator is allocated sufficient funds to permit him to stop a surveillance midstream and then gear up again to go back out. Mere suspicion that he is "made" does not usually stop the show.

Some would say the investigator should explain the risk of discovery before undertaking the job to forewarn the client that were he to continue after discovery, he risks, for them both, a claim of harassment, stalking, or intrusion into private space; each an ingredient of invasion of privacy.

As the cases teach, anyone making a fraudulent insurance claim, cheating on his or her spouse, stealing, or who is involved in any other illegal or immoral act should presume he or she is being watched by a private detective. That said, there is less patience shown by the courts with an intense surveillance when the target is patently free of wrongdoing. An investigator's actions are always judged on a sliding scale relative the subject's degree of wrongdoing. Aggressive surveillance in a dry well is asking for trouble.

In short, the investigator, a licensed professional bound by strict legal and ethical rules, is involved in a complicated interaction with the public.
He recognizes that surveillance can be harrowing to both himself and his subject, and complicated by the following issues:

– *Watch Communities*
It may not be possible to conduct or continue surveillance in Watch Communities under most circumstances. The

rights of neighbors must be respected and to alarm them is not a good thing. Contacting police before starting the surveillance is smart. While police may or may not cooperate, neighbors may be alarmed by unknown vehicles patrolling a closed community. Police cooperation is mandatory in Watch Communities. Usually police will cooperate fully with the PI's surveillance when his lawful purpose and identification are disclosed in advance; but not necessarily so. Either way, the PI must fully cooperate with police or risk confrontation in or near the subject's living area, which might disclose his presence and compromise his mission. Good judgment and ingenuity will invariably save the day.

– *Local Laws*
The investigator violates laws and ordinances at his own risk. Specifically, speeding, running lights, trespass, trash pulls, and video in private space can carry criminal sanctions and complaints to the licensing board.

The private investigator should adhere to the Rules of Safe Surveillance as further discussed in the author's book, *Navigating the Legal Minefields of Private Investigations* (Ron Hankin, Looseleaf Law Publications, Inc., 2008).

Rules of Safe Surveillance

Rule 1 – Stick to the Public Eye
What the subject does in the "public eye" is not protected; that is, in general, the private operative can observe, look, and listen from a place he has a right to be. The public eye means the action can be observed by other members of the public.

Rule 2 – Don't Trespass in Private Places
That is, don't trespass into the subject's dwelling, curtilage, or space that he reasonably expects is private.

Rule 3 – Don't Scope a Private Place
That is, don't use binoculars or high-powered zoom lens to view that which would not be observed without such enhance-

ment from a place you have a right to be. An off-the-shelf zoom lens with typical camera is acceptable.

Rule 4 – Don't Use the Bad Ruse

That is, don't use a pretext to gain entry into the subject's dwelling, curtilage, other space he reasonably expects is private, or where custom, usage, and common sense indicate one should steer clear of (e.g., abortion clinics, government installations, etc.).

Rule 5 – Don't Delve into Private Matters

That is, when on assignment, don't report private information to your client that is irrelevant to your mission.

Rule 6 – Don't Make a Pest of Yourself

That is, during any surveillance avoid continuing the surveillance when discovered or "burned"—give it up for the day. Be especially alert to actions taken by the subject to evade surveillance when you are discovered. This is possible harassment and actionable as invasion of privacy.

Each of the foregoing Rules of Safe Surveillance intertwines with the cases discussed in this book. The Rules constitute what is commonly referred to as "good judgment."

Case 2
Souder v. Pendleton (La., 1956)

Insurance claims manager Keyes dialed up PI Cannon about another claim, this one involving a woman with a sprained back. "Claims she tripped and fell up two steps!" Keyes said. "*Up*, I say, not down. How can you fall up stairs? She's lying—I can smell it—check her out."

On the first day out, Cannon thought he would start the investigation by "asking around." Perhaps a neighbor would save everyone a lot of trouble, by not only telling Cannon that the claimant, a Ms. Barnes, was able bodied, but maybe even help keep a future eye

Chapter Two   15

on her. Not an uncommon tactic when handled properly. Each detective has his own way of testing a neighbor for such a purpose. But slandering the claimant in one's first approach to a neighbor is a sure way to draw fire.

At a residence just a few doors down from that of the claimant, Cannon identified himself as a private investigator. He told the woman who answered the door, "Keep it under your hat, but we're watching your neighbor Barnes for suspected insurance fraud. Can you tell me anything about her physical condition?" The neighbor said, "Only that she's my sister," and shut the door in his face.

Cannon parked his car on the edge of Barnes's property where he could see right into the house. He even got out of the car and walked to the side of the house where he could get a better vantage point. Though he could make out some activity in one of the bedrooms, he needed binoculars to confirm it was the claimant moving around clothed only in her slip. He moved the binocular view from bedroom to bedroom when suddenly a man's face stared back at him in the viewfinder. Cannon hastily did a double take and ran for his car. Luckily, the engine started and he sped off, but none too quickly, as the man now was fast approaching wielding a broom. Cannon drove to the next block and parked: time to let his nerves settle before hatching another plot.

It was then a police squad car pulled up and blocked his exit. Two officers got out and Cannon met them, credentials at the ready. "Insurance fraud," he said. "Got reports of a cheat on the next street. I'm about to go back over there." The officers did not look happy. One officer took Cannon's credentials and carefully looked them over. "Mind if we search your vehicle?" the other asked. Cannon agreed. "Next time, better call us," he said, handing Cannon his rear car seat. Finally, Cannon got his credentials back, and was told to leave. As Cannon drove off, he mumbled to himself, "They should show more professional courtesy."

The next day he phoned the desk sergeant to notify him of a return to the area, but instead was told, "Get in here! We got complaints on you!" At the station, he was informed that police had received verbal complaints against him of trespassing, being a peeping tom, and stalking on the claimant's property. He was told to stay away or risk arrest. A few days later, Keyes's office was served with a summons of a civil suit for invasion of privacy, alleging harassment and stalking.

At trial, the judge made comment on the general rule that insurance companies must be given leeway to vigorously investigate all insurance claims. The judge said, "It is in the best interest of the industry and its customers. All claimants should understand that they will be watched closely for that purpose." He dismissed the case, but there was an appeal.

In a case with similar facts, on appeal to the Court of Appeals of Louisiana, the decision was reversed and the PI and the insurance employer were held liable. The Appeals Court said investigators must hold themselves to a high standard in watching other people or risk invasion of privacy.

Said the court:

The right of privacy has been defined as "the right to be let alone" and as "the right to live one's life in seclusion, without being subjected to unwarranted and undesired publicity." On the other hand, however, we must consider the right of our insurance companies to investigate any and all possible claims which might be filed against them. In the instant case, there was a possible suit for workmen's compensation benefits against the insurance company and its assured. We, therefore, feel that the insurance company and its agents, the detective agency, had a right to make such investigation as it deemed necessary, provided that such investigation was conducted within legal bounds.

Now the petition alleges that the investigation was conducted in such a manner as to harass, invade, and embarrass the petitioner. It further alleges that the detectives trespassed upon the property of petitioners, and peeked into their windows. Now, accepting as true, that the detectives trespassed upon the property of petitioners and peeked into their windows, it appears that the detectives might have been guilty of a crime under our 'Peeping Tom' statute [which] defines a 'Peeping Tom' as '* * * one who peeps through windows or doors, or other like places, situated on or about the premises of another for the purpose of spying upon or invading the privacy of persons spied upon without the consent of the persons spied upon. It is not a necessary element of this offense that the 'Peeping Tom' be upon the premises of the person being spied upon.'

... It certainly would follow that, if a possible crime was committed, a suit in civil damages would be present, provided that damages could be proved. We, therefore, feel that the petition did allege a cause of action, i.e., an invasion of the petitioners' right of privacy...

Souder v. Pendleton, 88 So2d 716 (La 1956)

2B: Stalking

Every state has a stalking law; although elements of the offense vary widely. In some jurisdictions, a repeat phone call after an initial warning may suffice. Many PI cases start with a 9-1-1 complaint of a suspicious vehicle following the caller. Police, not forewarned of an active PI operation, may aggressively respond with little tolerance for the PI's difficulties in conducting a one-car, one-man moving surveillance. The stage is set for a rhubarb. When the PI is cooperative but vague about his purposes—keep in mind that in some states it is illegal for the PI to reveal the name of his client or details of his investigation—the stage is set for a stalking charge.

Often the same facts that establish stalking make a tidy case of invasion of privacy. Anytime a PI is charged with stalking, he has the expensive task of proving he had a *lawful purpose*—that he acted within his statutory authority.

2C: Lawful Purpose

Few jurisdictions exempt the PI from their stalking laws on the basis of a license alone. In most states, the license is a starting point; in addition, there must be *lawful purpose*. An operative may be asked to satisfy police (or prove to the local prosecutor and court) that the surveillance in question was for hire and complied with his statutory authority of investigating the "habits, conduct, business occupation, honesty, integrity, ... movements, whereabouts ... (and) acts ... of any person, firm, association or occupation."

This feet-to-the-fire action of a PI by police is unusual, but it certainly happens when a tight surveillance puts the PI's target or someone in the general public in fear of life and limb. Because the facts that establish stalking may lay groundwork for a claim of invasion of privacy, the PI should abide by the Rules of Safe Surveillance previously discussed (see p. 13).

The gumshoe knows danger lurks with any surveillance—and lack of patience increases this risk exponentially. An experienced PI knows the harder the push, the greater the risk of failure.

Case 3
Nastal v. Henderson (Mich., 2006)

Keyes put down a file and dialed up Private Investigator Jack Heart. "Car hit from the side," Keyes said. "I never saw a case of whiplash where the claimant got hit from the side! Investigate!"

At the claimant's home, Heart observed the claimant drive off in his car. Heart followed. In a few miles, the claimant suddenly stopped his vehicle, got out of his car, and walked back to Heart's vehicle. Heart rolled down his window. "Engine stalled?"

Chapter Two

"No," said the claimant. "You following me?"

"No, absolutely not. Why would I do that?"

"Insurance company send you?"

"Hey, bub, you're imagining things. I'm an accountant driving to my next job."

The claimant returned to his car and drove off; and so did Heart, turning at the next corner. Things would have to cool before he went back out again. Two days later Heart, back at the claimant's residence, watched him carry an eighty-pound sack of topsoil from a shed and vigorously rake it level. Heart filmed the activity. The PI now had enough and submitted his report with video to Keyes. The claim was denied and the claimant sued. During pre-trial discovery, the claimant discovered that the driver he confronted on the street was in fact an insurance investigator. He amended his lawsuit to include a count of invasion of privacy based on stalking.

The trial court agreed with the claimant that the investigator had committed stalking. The lower court said that the investigator's lawful purpose of investigating an insurance claim *ended* when the claimant confronted the investigator. From that point on, after such discovery, any further surveillance by the PI constituted stalking and harassment.

In a case with similar facts, the investigator and his insurance company prevailed on appeal to the Michigan Supreme Court. The court held that the investigator was acting within his statutorily authorized authority and lawful purpose, and that there is nothing improper in an investigator's refusal to admit to an ongoing surveillance when confronted by his target.

Said the court:

Stalking constitutes a willful course of conduct whereby the victim of repeated or continuous harassment actually is, and a reasonable person would be, caused to feel terrorized, frightened, intimidated, threatened, harassed, or molested ... however, conduct that is constitutionally protected or serves a legitimate purpose cannot constitute harassment or, derivatively, stalking.

It is that safe harbor of "conduct that serves a legitimate purpose" that is the linchpin of this case. The defendants here, private investigators licensed pursuant to [law], are authorized to "obtain information with reference to any of the following":

(i) Crimes or wrongs done or threatened against the United States or a state or territory of the United States.

(ii) The identity, habits, conduct, business, occupation, honesty, integrity, credibility, trustworthiness, efficiency, loyalty, activity, movement, whereabouts, affiliations, associations, transactions, acts, reputation, or character of a person.

(iii) The location, disposition, or recovery of lost or stolen property.

(iv) The cause or responsibility for fires, libels, losses, accidents, or damage or injury to persons or property.

(v) Securing evidence to be used before a court, board, officer, or investigating committee.

Accordingly, surveillance, when it is conducted to obtain evidence concerning a party's claim in a lawsuit, is valid and well within the law. Indeed, once involved in litigation, such as here, it is even more reasonable, in fact predictable...that surveillance to secure or even lead to evidence is permitted "in order to narrow the range of disputed issues which might otherwise needlessly waste the parties' and judicial resources."

It is only when the surveillance ceases to serve or contribute to the purpose of securing the information permitted by [law] that conduct would be outside the statutory safe harbor ... and a civil action for stalking could be maintained. Here, [the lower court] incorrectly concluded that there was a genuine issue of material fact concerning whether defendants' surveillance ceased to serve a legitimate purpose once [the claimant] discovered it. [Whereas, the investigator testified that he] believed that further surveillance conducted at later times, especially after a cooling off period, could produce information useful to the case.

Surveillance by a licensed private investigator is conduct that serves a legitimate purpose as long as the surveillance serves or contributes to the purpose of obtaining information, as permitted by [law]. Thus, surveillance conducted for and contributing to such purposes is beyond the stalking statute. The conduct at issue in this case served a legitimate purpose even after plaintiff observed the private investigators following him. Accordingly, the judgment ...is reversed and the case is remanded to the circuit court for the entry of summary disposition in [the investigator's] favor.

Nastal v. Henderson & Associates Investigations, Inc., No. 125069 (MI 3/21/2006) (MI 2006)

2D: Ruse

The private detective finds himself involved in a myriad of high risk ventures to garner information and solve crimes. Without some leeway in how he accomplishes his assignment, he couldn't listen, watch, or report without breaking the law and/or impinging on someone's privacy. If he had to risk his personal estate at every turn, no one would want the job, and we know that is not the case. In fact, on the contrary, credentials of a private detective are highly sought after: it is a rare agency that does not receive frequent inquiries from highly qualified applicants offering to work for free to break into a lucrative and exciting profession.

The saving grace is that it is not the claimant/subject's subjective sensitivity of intrusion that sets the standard for invasion of privacy—it is that of the *reasonable person*. So, while a gumshoe's action may seem intrusive and unreasonable to his target, the PI's action usually passes muster with the arbiter that counts—the court.

Courts are inclined to cast an indifferent eye on the detective's innocent use of pretexts not meant to defraud or harm—just tricks to disarm his adversary so the "truth will come out." While these harmless tactics invariably offend the thin skin of any target, they are not offensive to the reasonable person provided they are used judiciously with a good dose of common sense. Included in the PI's arsenal of tricks is the ruse—a pretext, subterfuge, or "innocent con job." To be clear of privacy danger, the PI must distinguish between the Good Ruse and the Bad Ruse. And, without using those terms, so have the courts.

The Good Ruse
Courts view the typical ruse as necessary hardware in an operative's toolbox—done for a purpose and consistent with his legislative authority: we refer to this so-called *lawful purpose* as the Good Ruse (as further discussed in *The Legal Minefields of Private Investigations,* Ron Hankin, Looseleaf Law Publications, Inc., 2008).

The Good Ruse is an invaluable device used to gain entry to property otherwise closed to the PI—most often a semi-public place or event entered by invitation only. The Good Ruse is used to acquire information not protected by law providing the investigator's actions are not offensive to the reasonable person. A court's determination of what is reasonable is not based on the subject's ownership interest, but rather his reasonable expectation of privacy. Without such expectation, the detective can watch, listen, and report activities acquired through ruse or even trespass.

For instance, property and events closed to the general public, but open by invitation to select members of the public, are the workplace of private detectives. While the property or event in question may not be open to the detective personally, the group invited now includes the PI operative, who by ruse, fault of the gatekeeper, or other peaceful means has joined the festivities. This semi-public environment obviates a reasonable expectation of privacy.

Chapter Two 23

Case 4
Furman v. Sheppard (Md., 1998)

Claims manager Keyes selected a claim for investigation. The case involved a truck driver who claimed he fell off a loading dock and hurt his back. What cued Keyes's suspicions was a recent rash of truck drivers making the same claim: back injury sustained falling off a loading dock. Keyes guessed that one driver had hit a home run, so others, envious, wanted to copy. Keyes called in Jack Heart, a private investigator, to commence surveillance of the claimant. If the man was hurt, Heart would say so.

Heart drove over to the claimant's home and parked where he'd have a long-distance view of the house. He wouldn't park long because it was a Watch Community and he'd have to stay on the move. On one trip around the block he returned in time to see the claimant loading some gear in the trunk of his car; whereupon, he and a female companion drove off with Heart following. The trip went directly to a private boat club on a large lake. At the gate to the club, the guard stopped the claimant's vehicle, checked his pass, and waved him in. The gate was clearly posted, "Private Property: Members Only," so Heart did not try to enter.

Instead, Heart drove to the closest Walmart, a block away, where he bought white shorts, white hat, and white sneakers. Heart changed into the shorts in Walmart's restroom, put on the sneakers and hat, and returned to the boat club. He parked on a side street and walked to the entrance. The guard's head appeared through the shanty window. "Pass, please."

"Got a problem, officer," Heart said, acting breathless. "I dock a few doors down. My jib broke loose ... should be floating past your dock right now!"

The guard came out of the shanty, clipboard in hand. "Need a pass," he said. "This is a private club."

"Sir, I got no insurance and my boat is going to sink!"

The guard grimaced.

"I'll be quick."

The guard raised his clipboard. "Got a driver's license?"

Heart handed him his driver's license. The guard made some notes, and said, "You got five minutes."

Inside the gate, Heart stopped for coffee at the club's free refreshment stand. Cup in hand, he sauntered down the many rows of boats until he spotted the claimant and his lady on a dry-docked sailboat. Heart set down his cup long enough to adjust the video camera hidden in a fanny pack hanging at his belt buckle. He was just in time to catch the supposedly disabled claimant raising heavy sail, and watched in envy as he shimmied up a mast some six feet to clear a pulley. Heart had what he needed and headed back to the gate. The guard met him there. "Any luck?"

"It sank."

The guard, in sympathetic voice, said, "Just buy insurance, wait 30 days, then file a claim. Insurance company won't know the difference."

"Yeah, you're right," Heart said. "They're pretty stupid."

When videotape of the claimant and his boat folly rolled at pre-trial meetings, the claimant saw himself and his wife in full color. Unappreciative of the attention

Heart had given them at their private club, he and she filed suit for invasion of privacy, claiming that when Heart entered private property—a member's only club—on ruse, he invaded their reasonable expectation of privacy. "So what if he lied to get in?" said attorney for the insurance company. "There was no reasonable expectation of privacy at a boat club."

In a case with similar facts, the Appellate Court of Maryland agreed and verdict for the investigator and insurance company was affirmed.

Said the court:

According to [plaintiff], because (1) the yacht club was not a public place, and (2) the investigator trespassed onto an area in which [the claimant] had a reasonable expectation of privacy, an actionable intrusion occurred. [We disagree]. Maryland has adopted the following definition of intrusion: The intentional intrusion upon the solitude or seclusion of another or his private affairs or concerns that would be highly offensive to a reasonable person.

To determine whether the surveillance constituted an actionable intrusion, ... we ask whether there has been an intrusion into a private place or the invasion of a private seclusion that the plaintiff has thrown about his person or affairs. There is no liability for observing him in public places since he is not then in seclusion. If surveillance is "conducted in a reasonable and non-obtrusive manner, it is not actionable."

The fact that [the investigator] made the observations while trespassing ... does not establish a violation of any reasonable expectation of privacy. Not every trespass constitutes an unreasonable search or intrusion. A trespass "becomes relevant only when it invades a defendant's reasonable expectation of privacy." "[A]n individual's reasonable expectation of privacy reaches its zenith in the home." On the other hand, business and commercial enterprises generally are not as private as a residence ... although a club operated for a select clientele may not be public, 'the fact that the premises are maintained as a club with a membership policy is not conclusive in favor of the club. Failure to enforce limitations on admittance would warrant the conclusion that the persons operating the club had no reasonable expectations of privacy ...

The surveillance conducted by [the investigator] involved nothing more than observations of [the plaintiff] while they were on or near a yacht situated in a public waterway and in open view of the public. [Plaintiffs] were performing acts which were in public view to other members of the club and to people boating in the water. Working on a boat may be important to a tort suit, when the ability of Plaintiff to do heavy work is at issue, but it is scarcely such as would be an intrusion on Plaintiff's right to seclusion.

In this case, because [plaintiffs] were seen doing things that could be observed by non-trespassing members of the general public, the circuit court correctly dismissed their intrusion claims.

Furman v. Sheppard, 744 A2d 583 (Md 1998)

The Bad Ruse

There are, however, places where private entry by deception is forbidden by all courts and clearly actionable as invasion of privacy.

Case 5
Burns v. Masterbrand Cabinets (Il., 2007)

Investigator Ace Cannon parked down the street from the home of an insurance claimant, Jay Higgins. It was a routine investigation of a work-related injury case. Higgins, a janitor, alleged he was injured working for Mountains are Us, a mountain climbing training facility. He had been mopping at the top of the mountain when he stepped backward and slid down the two and one-half stories to an inflatable rubber moat. Higgins claimed torn knee cartilage. When Keyes heard the plastic mountain top was only twenty-five-feet high, he

Chapter Two

suspected the man's injuries were as inflated as the rubber moat. He assigned Cannon to check things out.

Cannon watched the Higgins's place of residence for a couple of days but never saw the claimant. On the third day, already sensing Keyes's impatience, Cannon decided he'd cut to the chase and use a ruse he had employed on several other occasions to great advantage. He walked up to Higgins's front door and rang the bell. The door opened and an elderly man on crutches peered out. Cannon asked, "Are you Mr. J. Higgins?" The man nodded he was. "Sir," Cannon said, "I'm here on official business. I've got a picture of a young girl I want to show you."

"What young girl?"

"She's missing and we're asking around about her. Can we talk inside?"

Without further adieu, Cannon brushed by Higgins and took a chair at the kitchen table. Higgins followed him, limping to the side of the table. Cannon opened his wallet and put a pocket portrait of a young woman on the table and said, "Say, Mr. Higgins, you wouldn't have a little tea or something cold to drink, would you? It's been a long day."

Higgins limped to the refrigerator and came back with a container. Cannon watched Higgins while the detective's fanny-pack camera recorded him. "Some limp you got!" he said. "You hurt?" Higgins said he might need surgery for a bad knee, that he was hurt at work. "What about the girl?" Higgins asked. "What's that got to do with me?"

"Not important," Cannon said. "Just a runaway. She'll turn up." Cannon finished his drink, put the picture back in his wallet, thanked Higgins, and left.

The investigator submitted his video and report to Keyes who agreed: the video did not warrant claim denial. However, eventually, a dispute did arise over other injuries claimed by Higgins not evident in the video, and it was then the attorney learned of Cannon's visit to Higgins. He immediately filed suit for invasion of privacy.

The trial court agreed with Higgins that Cannon's entry into the Higgins' home on pretext was an invasion of privacy and awarded judgment for Higgins. Cannon and the insurance company appealed.

In a case with similar facts, the Illinois Appellate court affirmed the lower court's decision on appeal. The investigator and insurance carrier were liable for invasion of privacy.

Said the court:

One who intentionally intrudes, physically or otherwise, upon the solitude or seclusion of another or his private affairs or concerns, is liable to the other for invasion of privacy, if the intrusion would be highly offensive to a reasonable person. Plaintiff alleges the intrusion was highly offensive and that he sustained anguish and suffering as a direct and proximate cause of [the investigator entering his home.] P]laintiff has [successfully] alleged ... elements of the tort ... (1) an unauthorized intrusion or prying into the plaintiff's seclusion, (2) the intrusion [was] offensive or objectionable to a reasonable man, (3) the matter upon which the intrusion occurs [was] private, (4) and the intrusion caused anguish and suffering.
Burns v. Masterbrand Cabinets, 874 NE2d 72, 77 (Ill 2007)

Case 6
Noble v. Sears (Calif., 1973)

In another case of misguided ruse, an insurance investigator, assigned to procure the name and address of the passenger riding in the claimant's vehicle at the time of an accident, thought he'd save investigative time by just asking the driver for the information. Normally, that would not be a problem. In fact, using ruse to get information is a stock tool in the PI arsenal. But—a big *but*—in the case in question the claimant-driver was hospitalized with serious injuries; and to ask her for the information, he'd have to see her in the hospital. In so doing, he'd have to ignore a Cardinal Rule of Ruse: *You never use ruse to enter private space, such as someone's house, or their hospital room.* In this case, regrettably, he told the reception desk, nurses, and ultimately the claimant herself that the claimant's own attorney had sent him.

When he got to her bedside and informed the claimant he was a member of her attorney's investigative team, she readily provided the name and address of her passenger together with details on her injuries. Later, her attorney learned of the deception and predictably filed suit on her behalf for invasion of privacy, arguing a hospital room is private space in which the patient has an expectation of privacy. The defense countered that there are too many people in and out of a hospital room to call it private and under such circumstances a patient occupying a hospital room can have no reasonable expectation of privacy. The judge agreed and dismissed the suit.

But, in a case with similar facts, on appeal to the 2d District Court of Appeals of California, the court reversed, holding the investigator's intrusion was invasion of privacy.

Said the court:

Defendant Pruitt, an investigator, was hired to assist in preparing the defense. The attorneys desired to take the deposition of a man named Bohm, who had accompanied plaintiff on her shopping trip. That effort was frustrated because plaintiff either could not procure or did not have an address for Bohm. In an effort to secure the address from plaintiff, an employee of Pruitt, named Lemon, gained admittance to a hospital room where plaintiff was confined and, by deception, secured the address. It is that alleged invasion, and Lemon's conduct while in the room, which form the basis for plaintiff's claim of injury.

Plaintiff argues that an 'unreasonably intrusive' investigation, which plaintiff has alleged in her sixth cause of action, is a tort for which damages are recoverable. We agree. Various courts have recognized that an intrusive investigation may give rise to a cause of action for damages. The Florida Supreme Court recognized that an investigation done by trailing and shadowing a claimant could amount to an actionable invasion of privacy, if it is unreasonably intrusive. A Georgia court also has held that an investigation done in a frightening manner may provide a cause of action against a detective agency. [And a] Louisiana court ... held that an investigation by detectives hired by an insurance company must be conducted within legal bounds and failure to investigate in a proper manner may amount to a cause of action for breach of privacy. In California, the Supreme Court has recognized, in dicta, that a private investigation may give rise to a cause of action for damages for invasion of the right to privacy ...

Therefore, we hold that an unreasonably intrusive investigation may violate a plaintiff's right to privacy. The theory of plaintiff's complaint, as set forth in the first cause of action (incorporated by reference into the sixth) is that she had, at least as against Sears, Pruitt, Lemon and respondent attorneys, an exclusive right of occupancy of her hospital room. Assuming that that theory is sustained by proof, the other conduct alleged against Lemon would seem to fall within the concept of unreasonably intrusive investigation.

Noble v. Sears, 109 CalRptr 269 (Cal 1973)

2E: Trespass

It is a criminal offense to trespass onto the property of another when the property has been posted or there exists prior warning to stay off. For a private detective, the act of trespass may cost him conviction, fine and other aggravation; but the trespass itself does not make a reasonable view unreasonable. Case law establishes that trespass is often irrelevant to that which the PI observes and hears—providing the position so acquired does not intrude into the subject's reasonable expectation of privacy; said another way, trespass is not the basis of invasion of privacy: the key to civil privacy invasion is whether the subject action intrudes into the subject's reasonable expectation of privacy sufficient to offend a reasonable person.

The issue then is not whether the ground on which the PI stands was reached with or without lawful permission, but rather whether what he views or hears from that location intrudes into a reasonable expectation of privacy offensive to the reasonable person. If the observation does not offend, for these purposes, the location is a place the PI has a right to be and perfectly acceptable. Generally, a reasonable expectation of privacy does not share ground with the *public eye*.

"Public Eye": When the view is accessible to the public—the *Public Eye*—the PI's position, whether gained by trespass or ruse, has no bearing on legality of the observation. As discussed in *Furman* (p. 23), entering a members-only club puts the investigator in a place where other persons with lawful access can likewise observe what the subject is about—thus, negating his reasonable expectation of privacy.

Case 7
McCain v. Boise Cascade (Or., 1975)

Ralph Khiner leaned over too far and fell into a mixing vat at the Wisconsin Glue Company. It took a few minutes before fellow employees realized Ralph had disappeared, and they hit the "off" button. Fortunately, the vat was only partially filled, but, by the time he was pulled back out, Khiner had sustained some burns and eyelid blepharitis (stuck eyelids). Khiner filed claim for permanent disability, and when his case came across the desk of claims manager Keyes, he was skeptical. He reasoned, "How could a man possibly be injured falling into something as soft as glue?" He called PI Jack Heart to check Khiner out.

When Heart arrived at Khiner's home, he noticed a large vacant side yard adjoining Khiner's property, which was perfect for viewing activities in and about the exterior of the claimant's house and yard. Heart's intention was not to look into the house but to observe only those activities occurring in open view. He crossed the field and took a position where he was hidden behind a tree, camera at the ready. At some point, Khiner emerged from a garage on a riding lawn mower. Heart was still filming when Khiner stopped the machine on the garage apron, and got underneath the machine to change the cutting blades. Later he saw Khiner push the machine into the garage with no sign of injury.

When Keyes saw video of Khiner's activities, he set up a compensation hearing to reduce claim benefits. The man was entitled to compensation but certainly not permanent disability. It was during this hearing that it came out that Heart's video had actually been taken while Heart stood on vacant land adjoining Khiner's property. The vacant land was private property and Heart had clearly trespassed to get the video. Khiner's attorney filed suit for invasion of privacy, claiming compensatory and punitive damages. At trial, the evidence showed that a person standing in the public street could have taken the same video as that taken by Heart. The garage was open to public view, using the natural eye. The trial court held that the trespass, without more, was irrelevant; and did not constitute an invasion into Khiner's reasonable expectation of privacy.

In a case with similar facts, on appeal to the Supreme Court of Oregon, judgment in favor of the investigator and insurance company was affirmed.

Said the court:

The general rule permitting recovery for [invasion of privacy] is as follows: "One who intentionally intrudes, physically or otherwise, upon the solitude or seclusion of another, or his private affairs or concerns, is subject to liability to the other for invasion of his privacy, if the intrusion would be highly offensive to a reasonable man." It is also well established that one who seeks to recover damages for alleged injuries must expect that his claim will be investigated and he waives his right of privacy to the extent of a reasonable investigation. If the surveillance is conducted in a reasonable and unobtrusive manner the defendant will incur no liability for invasion of privacy. On the other hand, if the surveillance is conducted in an unreasonable and obtrusive manner the defendant will be liable for invasion of privacy.

The issue before this Court is whether trespass upon another's homestead for the purpose of conducting an unauthorized surveillance gives rise to an action for violation of the right of privacy. We think trespass is only one factor to be considered in determining whether the surveillance was unreasonable. Trespass to peer in windows and to annoy or harass the occupant may be unreasonable. Trespass alone cannot automatically change an otherwise reasonable surveillance into an unreasonable one ... All the surveillance in this case was done during daylight hours and when plaintiff was exposed to public view by his neighbors and passersby.

Assuming that the trespass in this case was intentional there was no evidence of intent to harm, harass or annoy the plaintiff. The surveillance took place near the boundaries of plaintiff's property. The trespass was unlawful, but did not injure plaintiff, nor was it intended to injure him. We think the court properly withdrew from consideration by the jury the claim for punitive damages on account of the trespass.

McLain v. Boise Cascade Corp. 533 P2d 343 (Or 1975)

2F: Invasive Trespass

We know that a trespass can be irrelevant to a reasonable expectation of privacy, but not every trespass is harmless. Those that present a view not otherwise available to the public eye may very well invade privacy.

> **Case 8**
> **Miller v. Brooks (NC, 1996)**

John and Jane Doe had spent some good years together; but then things went sour. It seemed Jane was hopelessly addicted to old movies, especially those with Joan Crawford. When she quit her job during Joan Crawford week to watch multiple reruns of *Mildred Pierce*, John had had enough. One day he tossed his checkbook on the table and said, "Take what's in there and get out." John had owned the house prior to marriage, so, at a preliminary hearing in conjunction with his action for dissolution of marriage, the judge ruled the residence was excluded from marital property. Pending final disposition of property rights, Jane was ordered by the judge to vacate and give up all keys.

Jane did as told and turned in her keys, but she was not done with John. Later, in the hallway, her attorney collected additional fees and told her that if she could prove to the judge that there was more to the story than just Jane's love affair with Joan Crawford, perhaps the judge would sweeten the pot. For instance, if she could show John was at fault—"screwing around"— the judge might slant things her way. The lawyer suggested she hire a private investigator to do some digging. He gave her the name of Ace Cannon. He said Cannon was full of ideas.

"Plant a camera right over his bed!" Cannon told her. "I do it all the time." To Cannon, that idea made darn good sense. One spouse wanted to check up on the other in the marital home. Who could argue with that? What could go wrong? She liked the idea. "By the way," she said. "Do you know a locksmith? The judge took all my keys." Cannon said that was not a problem. He would pick the lock himself. On John's next business trip, Cannon and his client gained entrance to the house. He planted a video camera in the ceiling directly over the bed while Jane rifled through John's dressers and a desk. On John's return from his trip, the camera was rolling. John entered his bedroom, undressed and headed for the shower. When he finished his shower he sat on the bed toweling, but quickly noticed he was sitting in dust—drywall dust. He looked around, then up, and discovered a hole in the ceiling. Soon John's own private detective was playing the video captured by the camera, including test pictures that included Jane and a detective that John's investigator immediately recognized as Cannon. John filed suit against Cannon for invasion of privacy. Cannon lost and appealed.

In a case with similar facts, on appeal to the North Carolina appellate court, the judgment against the investigator was affirmed.

Said the court:

It is generally recognized that: [O]ne who intentionally intrudes, physically or otherwise, upon the solitude or seclusion of another or his private affairs or concerns, is subject to liability to the other for invasion of his privacy, if the intrusion would be highly offensive to a reasonable person.

Here, plaintiff's ... evidence shows that defendants invaded his home, indeed, his bedroom, and placed a hidden video camera in his room which recorded pictures of him undressing, showering, and going to bed. Plaintiff's evidence also shows that ... [the investigator] picked up plaintiff's mail ... on one occasion. Acts of physically invading a person's home and opening his personal mail are wrongs protected by this tort. Plaintiff had every reasonable expectation of privacy in his mail and in his home and bedroom. A jury could conclude that these invasions would be highly offensive to a reasonable person.

Although a person's reasonable expectation of privacy might, in some cases, be less for married persons than for single persons, such is not the case here where the spouses were estranged and living separately. Further, the marital relationship has no bearing on the acts of [the investigators]. Plaintiff's marriage ... did nothing to reduce his expectations that his personal privacy would not be invaded by perfect strangers. The acts of installing the hidden video camera and the interception of plaintiff's mail as alleged and forecasted are sufficient to sustain plaintiff's claims for invasion of privacy by intrusion on his seclusion, solitude, or private affairs.

Miller v. Brooks, 472 SE2d 350, 354-355 (NC 1996)

Chapter Three
PROCURING AND SELLING CONFIDENTIAL INFORMATION

When consistent with his statutory authority and lawful purpose, the private detective has credit company access to unpublished personal information that he can lawfully disseminate to his client. There are times, however, when this well runs dry and the PI must resort to his gumshoe heritage—talking to people and digging, using tricks of the trade.

Case 9
Keyzer v. Amerlink (NC, 2005)

Stanley Hack played viola for the Ashland County Orchestra. Anxious to move from a trailer park, he and wife Sandy bought a two-acre lot with prime waterfront frontage on the Chippewa River. Hack had always wanted the largest home in Butternut, his hometown, and a recent raise gave Hack the funds needed. He contracted with a company called North Woods Log Cabins for a kit home and hired a local contractor, Billy Jurges, to build the home.

In time, materials stacked up on the Hack property, but construction did not commence. Although it had been a particularly mild summer, with daytime temps never under 32 degrees, Hack saw no activity at the site. One day, he tracked down contractor Jurges at a local bar to complain. Jurges said there was nothing he could do. The materials that had been delivered did not match the plan. The plan called for two garage openings but he only got one door; and the plan specified two bedrooms and there was material for only one. He had called North Woods, the manufacturer, he explained, but all he ever got was voice mail.

Hack stormed out of the bar and headed to a local attorney, Melvin Parnell. Parnell said they had two choices: they could sue Jurges, his contractor, but Jurges was obviously incompetent and probably insolvent, or they could sue North Woods, a robust kit builder. Hack decided to sue North Woods. Some time later, the parties reached a pre-trial agreement: The suit would be dismissed with prejudice; North Woods would refund fifty-five hundred dollars of the purchase price in full settlement of the claim; and neither Hack nor attorney Parnell would disclose terms of the settlement to any third person for a period of five years. Were the terms to be disclosed, not only would Hack be liable to refund the settlement but would be assessed a twenty-five percent penalty. On Parnell's recommendation, they settled the case on that basis.

Meanwhile, North Woods's attorney had heard that Hack's attorney, Parnell, was a known boaster and heavy drinker. He believed, without much effort, Parnell could be made to disclose the settlement and amount. If Parnell did as expected, North Woods's attorney would get a refund of North Woods's money, penalties, and a fat fee for himself. He called in a private detective to help. The detective would approach Parnell in an effort to get him to discuss the settlement. The next day, the detective and an associate were sitting in metal stack chairs facing Parnell as prospective new clients. The detective explained that North Woods sold him a kit home but the construction instructions made no sense and there was zero factory support. Parnell asked, "Who sent you?" The detective said, "I met a guy in Scholz's bar the other night ... he said he had a similar situation to what I have with North Woods and you sued and they paid ... and paid big time."

"Scholz's bar, Glidden?"

"Yeah, right, the guy said you were a tiger. I didn't get his name."

"Hack! Did he tell you how much we got?"

"Just said a lot of money."

Parnell reached behind him and lifted a can of beer from a small refrigerator and popped the cap. "Had to be Hack!" he said. "He shouldn't shoot off his mouth like that." Parnell drank from the can and wiped his chin on his coat sleeve. "What I'm about to tell you is only between us girls. Yeah, I got North Woods for fifty-five hundred." He tapped the only file on his desk. "Yeah, got them good, and I can do the same for you. That company is really screwed up."

They talked about the case some more and the detective told the attorney he would get back to him. Soon, affidavits went out to the Hacks and Parnell alleging violation of the confidentiality agreement, with demand for refund of the settlement payment plus damages. Embarrassed he had been taken by a private investigator, Parnell filed suit for invasion of privacy.

At trial, Parnell claimed his office was private space and that a private investigator for North Woods had intruded into his seclusion, solitude, and private affairs. Parnell alleged a law office is off-limits to ruse. The trial court agreed that Parnell's private space had been invaded and awarded judgment.

In a case with similar facts, on appeal to the Court of Appeals the court reversed, finding for the investigator. The court held that under the circumstances presented, it was not improper to gain entry into the law office by pretext in an effort to dupe the lawyer into disclosing his client's file. The attorney had no authority to discuss his client's case with an unknown third person.

Said the court:

The tort of invasion of privacy by intrusion into seclusion has been recognized ... as the intentional intrusion "physically or otherwise, upon the solitude or seclusion of another or his private affairs or concerns ... [where] the intrusion would be highly offensive to a reasonable person." The kinds of intrusions that have been recognized under this tort include "physically invading a person's home or other private place, eavesdropping by wiretapping or microphones, peering through windows, persistent telephoning, unauthorized prying into a bank account, and opening personal mail of another."

Thus, generally, there must be a physical or sensory intrusion or an unauthorized prying into confidential personal records to support a claim for invasion of privacy by intrusion ... [In this case], plaintiffs fail to articulate how these allegations, if true, constitute evidence that any of their personal affairs or private concerns were intruded upon. Moreover, none of the plaintiffs produced any evidence, by affidavit or otherwise, that defendants had investigated their personal affairs; had spied on, observed, or otherwise obtained any information about their private concerns; had actually obtained any information protected by the attorney-client privilege; had entered personal, non-commercial, areas of any of their houses; or had in any other way involved themselves in any of the plaintiffs' private or personal lives.
Keyzer v. Amerlink, Ltd., 618 SE2d 768, 771-772 (NC 2005)

3A: Credit Information

For the private investigator, a luxury of the modern era is computer credit company services. These sources provide him "header" or "locate" information, including basic present and past addresses, unpublished telephone numbers, and other materials not contained in public documents such as a partial social security number useable for matches. This information is invaluable in locating individuals and for other lawful reasons consistent with the Fair Credit Reporting Act (FCRA).

Chapter Three   **41**

However, the FCRA prohibits procuring or selling information that might establish credit worthiness without a permissible purpose. Unlike a header, credit information goes to the heart of an individual's privacy: namely, his or her credit rating. But does a PI necessarily invade privacy in releasing such information when done in good faith?

> **Case 10**
> ***Phillips v. Grendahl* (8th Cir., 2002)**

Sally Waitkus had a sick feeling her son-in-law-to-be was not the man he claimed to be. Ralph Slick claimed he was a rich lawyer, but for reasons of his own preferred working out of a Nash station-wagon, rather than being "tied down to an office." Still, she did hold out hope that he was a rich lawyer; after all, he had demonstrated that he was rude, arrogant, and highly unlikable. So, to find out more, Sally decided to hire a private investigator. She called in Ace Cannon, PI.

At her first meeting with Cannon, Sally confessed she had started the investigation without him. She'd already gone through Slick's wallet and found his social security number. Using this information, Cannon got on his computer to order a "Finder's Report." He had been told at a recent investigator's class that a "Finder's Report" was just a search to help find someone, and, as such, was not regulated by the FCRA. That is, it was not a search to establish "consumer eligibility for new or continued credit, collections of an account, insurance, licensing, employment purposes, or otherwise in connection with a legitimate business transaction involving the consumer."

When Cannon got the Finder's Report, he was impressed with all the niceties the report contained. It listed past addresses, past income, payment obligations, debts, employment data, and an arrearage for unpaid child custody payments—all financial information. But Cannon had the course outline right in front of him and it confirmed a Finder's Report was an FCRA compliant. Accordingly, Cannon passed on to Sally the entire Finder's Report. In reviewing the stark details, Sally came out of her chair, astonished to learn of Slick's long list of creditors and sick financial condition. Lawyer or not, he was an obvious deadbeat and not about to marry her daughter. She confronted Slick and he hit the fan. When he learned what Sally and Cannon had been up to, digging for financial background on him, Slick displayed some definite lawyer traits: he started screaming and threatening a suit. In fact, he meant it and soon filed suit for invasion of privacy, claiming breach of the FCRA.

The trial court agreed with Slick that the investigator and Sally had violated the FCRA. The court said the so-called Finder's Report used in this case was, indeed, a document that qualified as a Consumer Report, and as such was regulated by the FCRA. The course materials were wrong. Thus, without permissible purpose, Cannon could not order financial background on a subject, let alone disseminate such findings. The court noted the litany of permissible purposes available to Cannon, but checking out a client's prospective son-in law without his permission was not one of them. Cannon had thus invaded Slick's privacy. The court awarded damages.

In a case with similar facts, on appeal to the 8th Circuit Court of Appeals, the court ruled for the private investigator and his client. While true that technically the investigator had violated the FCRA by disseminating credit information, his actions did not amount to action offensive to a reasonable person. In this instance, at least, the information procured, taken as a whole, was not offensive to a reasonable person; and, important to note, the private investigator had acted in good faith. It was shown he had taken a class on the subject to stay compliant with FCRA, but the FCRA is a complicated subject.

In separating the FCRA issue from invasion of privacy allegations, the court said:

[FCRA]

The Fair Credit Reporting Act, 15 U.S.C. §§ 1681b-1681u (2000), prohibits the disclosure of consumer credit reports by consumer credit reporting agencies, except in response to the following kinds of requests: (1) court order or subpoena (2) request by governmental agencies involved in setting or enforcing child support awards (3) request authorized in writing by the consumer about whom the report is made or (4) request by a person whom the reporting agency has reason to believe intends to use the consumer report for one of a number of specific, permissible business reasons [such as when used as a factor in establishing a consumer's eligibility for new or continued credit, collections of an account, insurance, licensing, employment purposes, or otherwise in connection with a legitimate business transaction involving the consumer]."

The first step in establishing liability ... for obtaining a consumer report without a permissible purpose is to show that the document at issue was a "consumer report." A consumer report must contain information "bearing on a consumer's credit worthiness, credit standing, credit capacity, character, general reputation, personal characteristics, or mode of living." The Finder's Report listed "Trade Line Information," consisting of the names of several creditors with whom Phillips had credit accounts and the existence of a child support obligation, with dates for "last activity," but no other details such as amount of obligation or payment history. The District of Columbia Circuit has held that information showing the existence of trade lines, even without any details of credit history, satisfies the minimal requirement that information "bear" on the subject's "mode of living," since it shows that he has bothered to establish credit accounts. The Finder's Report also lists Phillips's former employers, which also would bear on his mode of living by showing that he has been employed. We conclude that the Finder's Report contains the kind of personal information required by the definition of consumer report *[and its release without permissible purpose is illegal]*.

Investigating a person because he wants to marry one's daughter is not a statutory consumer purpose ... Even if getting married can be characterized as a consumer transaction, it was not *[the proposed mother in law]*, but her daughter, whom *[the groom]* was engaged to marry. He had no business transaction pending with *[the mother in law]*. There was no permissible purpose for obtaining or using a consumer report.

[Private Facts]
The tort of publication of private facts consists of giving "publicity to a matter concerning the private life of another ... if the matter publicized is of a kind that (a) would be highly offensive to a reasonable person, and (b) is not of legitimate concern to the public." "Publicity" ... means that the matter is made public, by communicating it to the public at large, or to so many persons that the matter must be regarded as substantially certain to become one of public knowledge.... . Thus it is not an invasion of the right of privacy ... to communicate a fact concerning the plaintiff's private life to a single person or even to a small group of persons ... There is no evidence the *[investigator gave the report to anyone but the proposed mother in law, so the]* publication of private fact claim fails.

[Intrusion]
The tort of intrusion upon seclusion has three elements: an intrusion; that is highly offensive to a reasonable person; into some matter into which a person has a legitimate expectation of privacy. Of the information that might be private, none was of a nature that would render its discovery highly offensive to a reasonable person. Although we have determined the Finder's Report was technically a consumer report, it was quite skeletal. The only information pertaining to credit was the existence of the four "trade lines" and the existence of one trade inquiry, with no adverse or positive information about these entries ... Discovery of the trade lines and trade inquiry does not rise to the level of being highly offensive.

The Finder's Report did contain [the plaintiff's] social security number ... Although social security numbers are private, they are available in a wide range of contexts in our society. We provide them to others continuously. Discovery of that number therefore does not fit the profile of intrusion upon seclusion.

The most sensitive information in the Finder's Report was the existence of a child support order, but the existence of a child support order...is "public information[.]"

The use of improper methods to obtain information, such as a request that violates the Fair Credit Reporting Act, does not necessarily make the acquisition of information highly offensive, if the information could just as well have been obtained by proper means.

The district court did not err in entering summary judgment for the defendants on this claim. We ... affirm the entry of judgment [for the investigator] on the Invasion of Privacy claim [but] remand for further proceedings [on the FCRA violation].

Phillips v. Grendahl, 312 F3d 357 (8th Cir 2002)

3B: Sale of Unpublished Information

The private detective has a tremendous responsibility to persons he does not know, has never met, and who have not paid him a dime. These are persons whom his extraordinary investigative power may put in danger of financial harm, physical injury, and even death. The PI's obligation to such persons is more than ethical and moral. A red flag should alert any PI when an unknown client, or a client he cannot vet, requests unpublished information about a third person.

But is the release of such information invasion of privacy?

Case 11
Remsburg v. Docusearch (N.H., 2003)

Private investigator Ace Cannon sat at his desk cleaning the barrel of his Smith & Wesson, Model 10, when the phone rang. The caller identified himself simply as Shades. He'd gotten Cannon's name from the phone book. Shades said he was putting together an album for his school entitled, "Where Are They Now?" and wanted to hire Cannon to find a classmate. Cannon complimented him on the originality of the title and said he'd be glad to help.

Cannon slid the Smith aside with thoughts of that month's rent. There might be forty or fifty old classmates whom Shades wanted to locate—let's see, at fifty per, there's the rent and then some. But Shades quickly broke the spell when he said, "I actually found all but one on my own." Smith cradled the phone on his shoulder, and began rummaging through his desk for some cartridges. "She's Edith Stanky," Shades said. "I know a lot about her, though, including date of birth and her current phone number, but I'd like her address for the album." Phone still cradled, Cannon loaded his revolver. "You got her number," he said. "Why not call her yourself?"

"That would be uncool," Shades said. "You see, I understand she's still single—and we used to go together ... You know, to be honest, it's a bit awkward. I'm highly successful and she ... well, let's put it this way, she was quite fetched with me. I don't want her to get any ideas, and think ... anyway, know what I mean?"

"Yeah, I think I understand," Cannon said, slipping the thirty-eight into his shoulder holster. "You don't want to get her excited."

"Well put," Shades said. "Say, you know your stuff! I don't want her excited. I just need the addresses—work and home. Will three hundred cover it?"

"Three hundred, yeah, that works for me!" Cannon sat up and pulled out a pen, ready to take notes. As Shades promised, Cannon found the three hundred dollars stuffed in his door chute later that afternoon.

Chapter Three

That night, Cannon ordered a computer search used to locate subjects: a header, which cost him ten dollars. But more than one "hit" came up, so he went back to Shades by phone to clarify which Edith Stanky he wanted. Shades provided him a middle-initial and the PI soon had a match. In turn, Cannon passed on to Shades the home address of Stanky but Shades, not satisfied, insisted on the work address.

They agreed on an additional fee of seventy-five dollars, which Cannon invoiced and immediately mailed to Shades. But now, Cannon had a problem. He had learned from past unfortunate instances that under federal regulations (specifically the FCRA), employment information, such as place of employment, was not available through credit search companies without a permissible purpose—and, while tracking down a high school classmate, albeit a common source of PI business, has on occasion had a noble purpose, school reunions are not a permissible purpose under federal regulations.

On the other hand, Cannon could still get such information the old-fashioned way. After all, he was a gumshoe. But, since he already had Stanky's phone number, rather than using shoe leather, he'd just let his fingers do the walking. That night he dialed Stanky's home phone number and a female voice answered.

"Hello."

"Ms. Stanky?"

"Yes."

"This is Target Flower Service. We have a rose delivery for you from an admirer—with instructions to deliver at work."

"Flowers?"

"Roses."

"Who from?"

"Card just says 'admirer' and instructions to deliver at work."

"Wow! Wonder who that could be?"

"Dunno, but probably wants everyone at work to see how valuable you are."

Stanky bit on the flattery and gave up the address, which Cannon passed on to Shades. Relieved to be done with the matter—Shades gave him the creeps—Cannon closed the file but placed a copy of the invoice for the additional fee he had mailed Shades in the "to collect" box.

A few days later, Shades went to Stanky's place of employment and parked outside. But she wasn't about to receive flowers. When her work day was finished, Edith Stanky stepped into the open air, and Shades was ready. He shot her with a ten-gauge shotgun, then turned the weapon on himself. She died instantly as did Shades, with Cannon's unpaid invoice in his breast pocket. The invoice read, "Fee to get work address of Edith Stanky."

That night Cannon watched the television news about a murder-suicide and heard the name "Stanky." He sat up. Then he heard the name "Shades" and had his confirmation: he'd never collect that last invoice he'd sent Shades. In time he realized he had larger problems, but wasn't sure which form they might take. He had heard Ms. Stanky's family had hired a lawyer and Cannon's invoice with Shades came up. He called his own lawyer and was told, for three hundred an hour, the lawyer would research his liability in the matter. Specifically, any problems with providing her work address to Shades. A day later, counsel called back to say he had found a 2003 New Hampshire case entitled *Remsburg v. Docusearch*, which answered all of Cannon's questions.

Here are the four questions asked by Cannon, as rephrased by the Remsburg v. Docusearch court:

1. *Under the common law, does a private investigator who sells information to a client pertaining to a third party have a cognizable legal duty to that third party with respect to the sale of the information?*

"*All persons have a duty to exercise reasonable care not to subject others to an unreasonable risk of harm ... Thus, if a private investigator's ... disclosure of information to a client creates a foreseeable risk of criminal misconduct against the third person whose information was disclosed, the investigator owes a duty to exercise reasonable care not to subject the third person to an unreasonable risk of harm. In determining whether the risk of criminal misconduct is foreseeable to an investigator, we [mention two] risks of information disclosure implicated by this case: stalking and identity theft.*

It is undisputed that stalkers, in seeking to locate and track a victim, sometimes use an investigator to obtain personal information about the victims. [Also] Identity theft, i.e., the use of one person's identity by another, is an increasingly common risk associated with the disclosure of personal information, such as a SSN.

The threats posed by stalking and identity theft lead us to conclude that the risk of criminal misconduct is sufficiently foreseeable so that an investigator has a duty to exercise reasonable care in disclosing a third person's personal information to a client. And we so hold. This is especially true when, as in this case, the investigator does not know the client or the client's purpose in seeking the information."

2. If a private investigator obtains a person's social security number from a credit reporting agency as a part of a credit header without the subject's knowledge or permission and sells the social security number to a client, does the individual whose social security number was sold have a cause of action for intrusion upon seclusion for damages caused by the sale of the information?

"A tort action based upon an intrusion upon seclusion must relate to something secret, secluded or private pertaining to the plaintiff. Moreover, liability exists only if the defendant's conduct was such that the defendant should have realized that it would be offensive to persons of ordinary sensibilities. 'It is only where the intrusion has gone beyond the limits of decency that liability accrues.'

In addressing whether a person's SSN is something secret, secluded or private, we must determine whether a person has a reasonable expectation of privacy in the number. SSNs are used to identify people to track social security benefits, as well as when taxes and credit applications are filed. In fact, 'the widespread use of SSNs as universal identifiers in the public and private sectors is one of the most serious manifestations of privacy concerns in the Nation.' [A] person's interest in maintaining the privacy of his or her SSN has been recognized by numerous federal and state statutes. As a result, the entities to which this information is disclosed and their employees are bound by legal, and, perhaps, contractual constraints to hold SSNs in confidence to ensure that they remain private. Thus, while a SSN must be disclosed in certain circumstances, a person may reasonably expect that the number will remain private.

Whether the intrusion would be offensive to persons of ordinary sensibilities [depends] on 'the degree of intrusion, the context, conduct and circumstances surrounding the intrusion as well as the intruder's motives and objectives, the setting into which he intrudes, and the expectations of those whose privacy is invaded.' Accordingly, a person whose SSN is obtained by an investigator from a credit reporting agency without the person's knowledge or permission may have a cause of action for intrusion upon seclusion for damages caused by the sale of the SSN, but must prove that the intrusion was such that it would have been offensive to a person of ordinary sensibilities."

3. When a private investigator obtains a person's work address by means of a pretext telephone call and sells the work address to a client, does the individual's work address support an action for intrusion upon her seclusion?

"In most cases, a person works in a public place. 'On the public street, or in any other public place, [a person] has no legal right to be alone.' A person's employment, where he lives, and where he works are exposures which we all must suffer. We have no reasonable expectation of privacy as to our identity or as to where we live or work. Our commuting to and from where we live and work is not done clandestinely and each place provides a facet of our total identity. Thus, where a person's work address is readily observable by members of the public, the address cannot be private and no intrusion upon seclusion action can be maintained."

4. If a private investigator obtains a social security number from a credit reporting agency as a part of a credit header, or a work address by means of a pretext telephone call, and then sells the information, does the individual whose social security number or work address was sold have a cause of action for commercial appropriation of his name against the private investigator for damages caused by the sale of the information?

"An investigator who sells personal information sells the information for the value of the information itself, not to take advantage of the person's reputation or prestige. The investigator does not capitalize upon the goodwill value associated with the information but rather upon the client's willingness to pay for the information. In other words, the benefit derived from the sale in no way relates to the social

or commercial standing of the person whose information is sold. Thus, a person whose personal information is sold does not have a cause of action for appropriation against the investigator who sold the information."
   Remsburg v. Docusearch, 816 A2d 1001 (NH 2003)

Chapter Four
DISCLOSING PRIVATE FACTS

In many occupational endeavors, the pay is high with little risk and little work. Private investigators are not that lucky. A PI's remuneration is usually tied to high risk and hard work. If the PI can prevail and catch the miscreant in action, and not get shot or sued in the process, the bottom line can be handsome. It is this potential for high reward that prompts detectives to go beyond the call of duty. In the case that follows, hired to go undercover to ferret out thievery and illegal drug use at a local warehouse, information soon found hard to come by, the investigator began reporting personal information he thought might interest management to justify his invoices. Management was more than receptive.

But was it invasion of privacy?

Case 12
Johnson v. K-mart (Ill., 2002)

A retail chain had been hit with a spate of vandalism, thefts, and reports of rampant drug use in its warehouse distribution center. A private investigator was hired to infiltrate the operation and report back with the names of those involved. At some point it was anticipated the detective would provide evidence needed for wholesale terminations. Management placed the investigator in its warehouse workforce as a cargo handler. A female detective would assist him, working as a janitor's assistant. Only upper management would know of the caper.

After a few weeks, however, the investigator had nothing to report in the way of thievery or drug use. To that point, there was not enough criminal activity to justify the rather hefty fee he was charging management. Still, he was encountering considerable intelligence of another nature, information he thought might be of good use in the right hands. For instance, among the tidbits, he learned from talk in the lunchroom that a senior pallet driver was quitting without notice in a week to join a competitor. And he heard that an office supervisor was having an extramarital affair with her stock boy. While this was not the type information he was hired for, it would have to do.

The PI reported this mixed bag of rumor and fact to management, and like a hungry lion, management gobbled it up. A meeting of company management was called to take action based on what had been learned. The meeting included an assistant personnel manager who had not been privy to the undercover operation. When he heard the facts of what was being disclosed, he expressed extreme concern and suggested that some laws were being broken. His comment not only dampened the spirit of upper management, which wanted to use the information, it got him terminated the next day—albeit for some unrelated reason. It was then that the head of the local union received an anonymous phone call that "rats were loose" in the warehouse. The PI and his assistant were identified as undercover investigators. In short order, the assistant disclosed the entire operation, which led to the next step, the union filing suit on behalf of its membership claiming invasion of privacy; specifically, intrusion and disclosure of private facts. At trial, the private investigator and company management were found liable for heavy damages.

In a case with similar facts, on appeal to the Illinois Court of Appeals, the court affirmed the judgment. The court discussed the privacy issues involved.

Chapter Four

Said the court:

[As to] Intrusion upon Seclusion [invasion of privacy]:
  It is true, as defendant argues, that plaintiffs willingly provided these personal details to the investigators. However, we believe that the means used by defendant to induce plaintiffs to reveal this information were deceptive. Specifically, we believe that the act of placing private detectives, posing as employees, in the workplace to solicit highly personal information about defendant's employees was deceptive. A disclosure obtained through deception cannot be said to be a truly voluntary disclosure. Plaintiffs had a reasonable expectation that their conversations with "coworkers" would remain private, at least to the extent that intimate life details would not be published to their employer.
  The evidence presented shows that defendant placed undercover investigators posing as employees in the plant to obtain information regarding theft, vandalism and drug use at the plant. The evidence further shows that along with this information, the investigators compiled information regarding employees' family problems, health problems, sex lives, future work plans, and attitudes about defendant and reported this extremely personal information to defendant. The investigators gathered this information not only on defendant's premises, but also outside the workplace at social gatherings. The investigators testified that they included anything and everything that they heard in their reports. Defendant admitted that it had no business purpose for gathering information about employees' personal lives. Yet, defendant never instructed the investigators to change their practices or to stop including the highly personal information in their reports. We find that a material issue of fact exists regarding whether a reasonable person would have found defendant's actions to be an offensive or objectionable intrusion.

Publication of Private Facts [disclosure of private facts]:
  In the instant case, the facts at issue were clearly private. They included such things as employees' family matters, health problems, and sex lives. This highly

*personal information was acquired through a deception and then reported to plaintiffs' employer. We believe that an issue of fact exists regarding whether a reasonable person would find it highly offensive that these personal matters were made public to his employer. We next consider the publicity requirement. We too hold that the public disclosure requirement may be satisfied by proof that the plaintiff has a special relationship with the "public" to whom the information is disclosed ... The evidence shows that personal details about plaintiffs' private lives were disclosed to their employer by the investigators. We find that these facts raise a genuine issue as to whether publicity was given to private facts.
Johnson v. K-Mart,* 723 NE2d 1192, 1197-1198 (Ill 2002)

Chapter Five
FALSE LIGHT

A private investigator's verbal or written report to his client can be as dangerous to his financial future as any botched surveillance. He must ensure that reports are marked confidential and warn against further dissemination. One of a myriad of things that can trip up a PI is letting down his guard by confusing a third person with his subject.

But is it invasion of privacy?

Case 13
Association Services, Inc. v. Smith
(Ga., 2001)

A new claim caught the eye of claims manager Keyes. An office clerk married to the owner of the company claimed she slipped at work and sought workmen's compensation benefits. Keyes often checked the claims of disability by relatives of the owner. He had a hunch an investigation would find the relative drawing insurance compensation while still working. He called in Ace Cannon, private investigator, to check things out.

With only the claimant's description on hand, "white female about 40, red hair and weight in excess of 200 pounds," Cannon felt confident he would have no trouble identifying her. He drove to the claimant's home, saw no activity, and, as Keyes had suggested, continued on to the claimant's place of employment, the company owned by her husband. What he saw there confirmed Keyes's suspicion. The claimant, dressed in sweat clothing, was working near the front entrance arranging flowers. She appeared able bodied with no sign of injury. He followed the woman to a local

Home Depot where she bought more plants for the office before returning to the office for more planting. Cannon had seen enough and presented a video and report to Keyes.

"I knew it!" Keyes said. "Double-dipping."

Keyes denied the claimant's workmen's compensation claim; whereupon, the claimant's attorney demanded a meeting. More than happy to confront him with evidence of fraud, Keyes agreed to meet with the attorney and his client. When the claimant entered the office she walked in obvious pain. How convenient, Keyes thought. When Keyes rolled the video, he expected the claimant to squirm. Instead, she simply said, "That's Angelina."

"Angelina?" Keyes asked. "Who's Angelina?"

"My twin sister! She's the company landscaper."

Her statement was proven true. Keyes apologized to the attorney and offered to immediately withdraw his effort to stop benefits. Not enough. He even offered to pay the attorney for his time. But this offer too was rejected. Instead, the claimant and her sister filed suit claiming invasion of privacy based on the tort of False Light. Keyes had never heard of "false light" so he consulted with his own counsel and got the bad news. When Keyes and his investigator accused the wrong person of defrauding the insurance company, the erroneous accusation embarrassed both the claimant and her sister, and both now were possibly entitled to damages. Hopefully, Keyes's attorney said, the report went no further.

At trial, counsel for Cannon argued he had only the claimant's rough description to go by in the identification. He could not very well call her up and ask for a picture when he was investigating her. In addition, counsel reminded, there was no harm done. The PI's report was confidential and went no further than Keyes at the insurance claim department. The judge agreed and dismissed the case. The claimant and her sister appealed.

In a case with similar facts, on appeal to the Appellate Court of Georgia, the dismissal of the suit was affirmed.

Said the court:

Publicity which places plaintiff in a false light in the public eye is another of the four torts that make up the general tort of invasion of privacy. In a false light case, "[t]he interest protected is clearly that of reputation, with the same overtones of mental distress as in defamation." Essentially, to establish a claim of false light, a plaintiff must establish the existence of false publicity that "depicts the plaintiff as something or someone which [she] is not." Next, the plaintiff must demonstrate that "the false light in which [she] was placed would be highly offensive to a reasonable person." "[T]he hypersensitive individual will not be protected". Smith [the sister] argues that she was depicted in a false light by the videotape made by the detective, who mistakenly believed he was observing [the comp claimant] Pierce. Contrary to Smith's argument, however, we conclude that the undisputed evidence precludes her recovery on this claim.

First, Smith has not been placed in the public eye. Even though the tape was played in a conference room there is no evidence that any members of the general public saw the tape or even were aware of it. The investigators and the representatives of [the insurance carrier] viewed the tape in connection with their investigation of Pierce's claim. Unlike cases in which a plaintiff is falsely depicted in a televised newscast or in published materials, [this case is] devoid of any evidence of publicity.

Even assuming, arguendo, that the depiction of Smith in the videotape did publicly place her in a false light, we cannot conclude that the false light in which Smith was placed would be "highly offensive to a reasonable person." Any false depiction was merely the result of [the investigator] mistakenly recording Smith instead of Pierce. [We] do not find that the videotape of Smith would be "offensive and objectionable to a reasonable person of ordinary sensitivities." Accordingly, the trial court did not err in granting [the investigator's] motion for summary judgment as to Smith's claim of false light invasion of privacy.

Association Services v. Smith, 549 SE2d 454 (Ga 2001)

PART TWO: POLICE

Chapter Six
THE REASONABLE EXPECTATION OF PRIVACY

Evidence procured by a governmental agent such as a law enforcement officer in violation of the Fourth Amendment is inadmissible in court against the suspect; and the process by which the evidence was procured may also be actionable as the tort of invasion of privacy.

The Fourth Amendment reads, in part:

"The right of the people to be secure in their persons, houses, papers, and effects, against unreasonable searches and seizures, shall not be violated, and no Warrants shall issue, but upon probable cause, supported by Oath or affirmation, and particularly describing the place to be searched, and the persons or things to be seized."

When does the police search violate the Fourth Amendment? Generally, any police search conducted without a warrant or an approved warrant exception violates the Fourth Amendment *if* the defendant displays a reasonable expectation of privacy in the subject of the search. Lacking the requisite reasonable expectation of privacy, a warrant or warrant exception is not required. In fact, the police action in such an event amounts to a non-search—and the evidence admissible.

To understand the parameters of search authority vis-à-vis privacy, police are guided by the 1967 U.S. Supreme Court case of *Katz v. United States* (389 U.S. 347). *Katz* changed Fourth Amendment protections from protecting a place—that is, a government intrusion into a place where the defendant may have hidden evidence or contraband—to a protection of the defendant's "reasonable expectation of privacy" in the person, place, or thing searched.

Katz changed how courts look at the issue of privacy: no longer was the concern of courts to protect against the search of an individual's horse stable where he might have hidden secrets—instead, the focus became whether his expectation of privacy in hiding secrets in the horse stable was reasonable.

To earn this Fourth Amendment privacy protection, a defendant must pass a two-part test: (1) the defendant must display a subjective expectation of privacy; and (2) the expectation must be one society is willing to accept as reasonable. So, "… what a person knowingly exposes to the public, even in his own home or office, is not a subject of Fourth Amendment protection." But, once he does achieve this expectation of privacy, the police officer must provide a warrant or an approved exception to search.

6A: Warrant, Exceptions, and Non-Search: There are several alternative outcomes to any warrantless police action when a subject claims he is victim of an illegal search:

1. The court can find that police conducted a reasonable search based on an exception to the warrant requirement of the Fourth Amendment; or
2. the court can determine that the search was illegal; that is, a violation of the Fourth Amendment based on the officer having neither a warrant, nor approved exception, and that the action intruded into the subject's reasonable expectation of privacy; or
3. the court can determine the police action involved was not a search at all; that the Fourth Amendment did not apply because the subject lacked a reasonable expectation of privacy in the person, place, or thing searched.

Our interest here is not whether the seizure of contraband or other search effort fell neatly into some exception to the warrant requirement, option one (we leave that to another book: *Navigating the Legal Minefields of Private Investigations,* Ron Hankin, Looseleaf Law Publications, Inc., 2008); rather, our concentration is the second and third of the above options: whether the police action involved was an illegal search under circumstances typically preceding invasion of privacy claims; or, whether police action qualified as a non-search. Accordingly, what piques our interest here are cases with potential for claims of invasion of privacy.

Claims of invasion of privacy are not limited to private detectives or store security. On the contrary, police can be sued for invasion of privacy, their exposure perhaps broader in light of *The Federal Civil Rights Act, 42 U.S.C. Sect. 1983. Sect.1983* (CRA). The CRA allows victims federal redress when their state venue is inadequate to provide for police misdeeds.

The CRA also entangles private operatives, security personnel and private detectives, who act in concert with police; for instance, when, by agreement with police, private operatives arrest, interrogate, search, or hold suspects for police booking. In these instances, the private operative runs the risk of having claims of invasion of privacy, false arrest, and other tort actions litigated in federal court.

Chapter Seven
PRIVATE SECURITY

Private security act with considerable police-like authority, but they are not police and are not bound by the Fourth Amendment. While private security do not arrest, they "detain," under certain state statutes covering retail theft and other authorities with force necessary to hold the suspect until police arrive. They detain a suspect on the grounds of *reasonable suspicion,* the equivalent of probable cause; "an honest suspicion, that the subject committed the offense [in question]." (*Gontarez v. Smitty's Super Value,* 680 P2d 807, 812, Ariz., 1984.)

Case 14
Gillett v. Texas (Tx., 1979)

An undercover female security guard at Hoxie's Department Store knew what to look for: any shopping bag, large purse, or clothing not the customer's size taken into a changing room was the sure red-flag of shoplifting. The customer may as well have carried a sign reading, "I'm a retail thief!" In this case, the guard watched a slender female customer take a triple-X sweater off a rack and go into a changing room. She shut the curtain behind her. On the wall outside the room were signs posted that read, "Under surveillance by female security" and "We prosecute shoplifters."

The guard entered the adjoining changing room and dropped to her knees so she could see under the customer's partition. She watched as the customer slipped the oversized garment into her purse, adjust her clothing, and exit the room. The guard followed the customer past the checkout counter when she stopped her. "You're busted!" she said. "Let's have the sweater." After a scuffle, the customer was restrained and marched into a security office for police booking.

Now a defendant against charges of retail theft, the customer argued that the guard's peek under the partition wall was blatant violation of the Fourth Amendment; that anything she saw in the privacy of a changing room was invasion of privacy.

The prosecution countered that there can be no reasonable expectation of privacy in a store changing room; especially when the room is posted as being under surveillance; and without an expectation of privacy, there is neither a violation of the Fourth Amendment nor an invasion of privacy. The trial judge agreed and the customer was convicted. She appealed.

In a case with similar facts, on appeal to the Court of Criminal Appeals of Texas, the shoplifting conviction was upheld.

Said the court:

It is not necessary to pass on th[e issue of the Fourth Amendment] in this case because we hold that no right to privacy has been violated. What people seek to preserve as private, even areas accessible to the public, may be constitutionally protected by the Fourth Amendment. Further, areas such as public toilet stalls are private to the extent they are offered to the public for private, although temporary, use. Such constitutional protection, however, extends only to the limits that the design, purpose and plan of the public facility affords so that, when the design is such that there is no right to expect absolute privacy, there can be no invasion of privacy.

In the present case, the posted sign on the mirror which would under nearly all circumstances be looked at by female occupants of a fitting room was notice that one could not expect privacy. This room was for use by the public on conditions established by the business. If appellant did not want to use the fitting room under the posted conditions, she was not compelled to do so. Her testimony that she did not see the sign did not have to be believed by the trial judge. The same is true about her testimony concluding that she expected privacy.

In short, [the department store] did not have to furnish her a place so that she could commit theft in private.
Gillette v. State of Texas, 588 SW2d 361, 363-364 (Tex 1979)

But when private police act in close concert with governmental agents such as law enforcement they run the risk of falling under the specter of "color of law." Under this concept, private security face sanctions of the Fourth Amendment, just as though they were governmental agents, and damages for invasion of privacy.

Case 15
State v. Buswell (Minn., 1990)

There had been a rash of vehicle accidents outside the Smokey Mountain Raceway. The local sheriff thought the reason was that fans were leaving high on drugs. He devised a simple solution. He ordered the track's private security guards to search suspicious persons and vehicles as they entered the track for contraband drugs. Anyone caught with drugs would be held by private security until his county deputies could collect them for booking. The sheriff instructed the track's head of security to take appropriate action.

Before the next race, the head of security informed his security personnel that they now had "police authority to search all incoming persons and vehicles and if drugs are found, hold the subjects for booking."

When the track gates opened, a beat-up RV pulled up first. The guard noticed a tattoo on the driver's arm and ordered him out of the vehicle. "What up?" the driver asked. The guard replied, "I'll ask the questions. Get out here." The driver and vehicle were searched and a small quantity of cannabis discovered. The driver was handcuffed to a cyclone fence, and was soon joined by another driver, and finally a third. The three stood in the hot sun until deputies arrived to book them on charges of possession of illegal drugs.

At trial, the defendants argued the search of their person and vehicles was in violation of the Fourth Amendment: Security had neither a warrant nor warrant exception for the search. Since the defendants had a reasonable expectation of privacy in their person and vehicles, any evidence procured was inadmissible.

The prosecutor argued that private security officers are private citizens and private citizens are not bound by the Fourth Amendment. Therefore the case did not involve the Fourth Amendment. He argued that whether the drivers had a reasonable expectation of privacy was irrelevant to admissibility of the evidence. If the search and seizures were without reasonable suspicion, the defendants had redress in a civil court, but the evidence was admissible in a criminal case.

The trial court found the defendants guilty, but they appealed.

In a case with similar facts, the Court of Appeals of Minnesota reversed, holding that the gate searches were in violation of the Fourth Amendment and any evidence seized, inadmissible in court. With no evidence, the case was dismissed.

The court held that track security had become agents of the state when they agreed to perform police functions. The defendants had a reasonable expectation of privacy in their person and vehicles, and since the guards operated without a warrant or warrant exception, the searches and arrests were illegal.

Said the court:

It is well-settled that the Fourth Amendment applies only to governmental action ... The difficulty often arises, however, as it does here, in determining when governmental action occurs. There is no single authority directly bearing on this issue ... The test * * * is whether [the private citizen], in light of all the circumstances of the case, must be regarded as having acted as an 'instrument' or agent of the state * * *.

Case law identifies several determinants of public involvement. Our consideration of these factors leads us to the conclusion that the searches in the present case were public. As these factors are examined here, we review the record with respect for the additional rule of law that appellants have the burden to show by a preponderance of evidence that the security searches here were not private in nature.

- **Official Police Involvement**

    In the instant case, a meeting occurred where public officials and private security personnel reached an understanding regarding arrest procedures to be utilized upon the discovery of contraband by the private guards. Although this meeting dealt with the aftermath of searches, and not the manner of searching, the meeting produced a standing arrangement for contacts by the supervising security agent with police during the hours of operation, and a police officer was designated on call to assist with arrests.

- **Service of Public Policing Function**

    Private security guards may share with police an interest in public prosecutions premised on the results of a private search. Here, as already pointed out, the interest of the police was demonstrated in the prior meetings ... regarding the procedures to be used. Where some pre-search contact between the private party conducting the search and a potentially interested government official is shown, influence may be inferred. The security guards were clearly aiming at discovery of contraband and public prosecution of offenses thus discovered. This was so notwithstanding any private interest in controlling drug-induced misconduct.

- **Boundaries of Reasonable Private Policing**

    When intrusion goes beyond a reasonable and legitimate means for protecting private property, the *practice suggests a need for constitutional protection of individual liberty. The public does not reasonably anticipate, we conclude, a private prerogative for random searches, a regular part of admission to a public event, which are more intrusive than permitted for police authorities.*

In sum, we observe a combination of factors requiring the conclusion that the activity of private security personnel in this case took on a public character. There was significant official police involvement as indicated by the pre-search meetings between [the owner of the security company] and law enforcement officials.
Because the trial court concluded the search was private, it did not address evidence and argument on the fourth amendment issue. On remand, the trial court must weigh the issues for unreasonableness in the search activity, including consent for the scope of the search and the question of whether any contraband was found in the agent's plain view. Reversed and remanded.
State v. Buswell, 449 NW2d 471 (Minn 1990)

Chapter Eight
BODY SEARCH

A police search conducted without warrant or warrant exception may invade a reasonable expectation of privacy. While it may seem improbable that a person can claim a reasonable expectation of privacy for events occurring in a public street, consider a search in which the officer requires portions of the suspect's clothing be removed. Claims of intrusion into a reasonable expectation of privacy are made easier when the officer touches the opposite sex during a strip search, but just looking may also qualify.

Case 16
Hidey v. Ohio State Highway Patrol
(Ohio, 1996)

A state highway trooper clocked a white Olds going five miles over the speed limit. The trooper hit his siren and sped out from behind a highway sign trying to catch the Olds before someone got hurt. The Olds pulled onto the shoulder and the officer, on full alert, cautiously approached the vehicle. He would later say he became suspicious of the vehicle when he noticed its occupants "moving around a lot in their seats." Sensing, by their "erratic behavior," danger afoot, he ordered the occupants to "get out of the vehicle." The male driver and female passenger exited the car and he ordered the driver to lie flat on the ground. Next he told the female passenger to raise her shirt. When she asked why, he answered, "I'm checking for drugs." The girl did as ordered.

Finding nothing of an evidentiary nature to that point, next he ordered her to pull her panties away from her buttocks so he could "check things out." When she seemed to have difficulty doing this simple act, he tried to help, pulling on her panties so he could see her "sitting area." Still not finished, he took a flashlight and looked down the front of her panties. Again, coming up empty, he ordered her into the rear seat of his squad car.

With the girl in the back seat, the officer slid into this front seat and turned to face her. "I saw a lump in your shirt ... unbutton your shirt and show me what's in there." He had already looked under her shirt so she assumed he now meant that she should open her brassiere. Too frightened to disobey, she did as ordered. Once again, the trooper found nothing of evidentiary value. Done with the search, he told her to get dressed and the driver to get off the ground. He gave the driver a speeding ticket and sent the two on their way.

Two years passed but the girl forgot neither the incident nor the trooper's name. Now, claiming she was traumatized, she filed suit against the state police and the officer for invasion of privacy (his looking at her private parts) and battery (his touching her). At trial, the court threw the case out saying she had missed the one-year statute of limitations covering battery. The trial court disregarded the claim of invasion of privacy.

She appealed. In a case with similar facts, the Supreme Court of Ohio reversed.

Said the court:

The Supreme Court of Ohio has recognized ... [as invasion of privacy] the wrongful intrusion into one's private activities in such a manner as to outrage or cause mental suffering, shame, or humiliation to a person of ordinary sensibilities. [The tort] is set forth in the Restatement of Law 2d, Torts (1965) 378, Section 652B. Section 652B [which] states:

"*One who intentionally intrudes, physically or otherwise, upon the solitude or seclusion of another or his private affairs or concerns, is subject to liability to the other for invasion of his privacy, if the intrusion would be highly offensive to a reasonable person."*

*"Nor is there liability for observing him * * * while he is walking on the public highway, since he is not then in seclusion, and his appearance is public and open to the public eye. Even in a public place, however, there maybe some matters about the plaintiff, such as his underwear or lack of it, that are not exhibited to the public gaze; and there may still be invasion of privacy when there is intrusion upon these matters."*

Here, one can argue that [the deputy's] act of pulling appellant's pants away from her body could constitute an offensive touching. However, [he] did more than that. He shined a flashlight down the front of appellant's pants in observation and down the back of her pants, observing her buttocks. These acts do not constitute an offensive touching; they constitute an intrusion upon appellant's seclusion.

Even more telling is the conduct of [the deputy] requiring appellant to unbutton her blouse and expose her bra and left breast to him. This also consists of an intrusion into appellant's seclusion. Indeed, there was no touching or contact at all in this last act ... The true nature of the acts described in appellant's complaint is an intrusion upon appellant's seclusion. What is underneath her clothing is private and a part of appellant's seclusion. The intrusion upon these private matters, especially while on the side of an interstate highway, would be highly offensive to a reasonable person, and, indeed, appellant averred that those acts caused her humiliation, embarrassment, and mental distress. Had [he] stopped his conduct at the pulling of appellant's pants and underwear away from her body, the true nature of the acts may have been merely an offensive touching. However, [he] looked in her pants and at her buttocks. Without touching appellant, he required her to expose her bra and breast to him. The true nature of these acts was invasion of privacy. Therefore, the statute of limitations for appellant's invasion of privacy claim is four years.

Judgment ... reversed.

Hidey v. Ohio State Highway Patrol, 689 NE2d 89 (Oh 1996)

Chapter Nine
SCHOOL SEARCHES

The paternal aspect of school environment presents a unique Fourth Amendment variation: parents for the day, school officials have a "special need" exemption providing much more leeway to search than that provided police. The Fourth Amendment is bent to accommodate this special need, replacing probable cause of criminality with a variation, a simple "reasonableness test" in cases of "individualized suspicion." This test has been described by one court as follows:

"[F]irst, one must consider "whether the ... action was justified at its inception" ...; second, one must determine whether the search as actually conducted "was reasonably related in scope to the circumstances which justified the interference in the first place[.]" Under ordinary circumstances, a search of a student by a teacher or other school official will be "justified at its inception" when there are reasonable grounds for suspecting that the search will turn up evidence that the student has violated or is violating either the law or the rules of the school. Such a search will be permissible in its scope when the measures adopted are reasonably related to the objectives of the search and not excessively intrusive in light of the age and sex of the student and the nature of the infraction." *Joye v. Hunterdon Cent. High School,* 826 A2d 624, 658 (2003).

However, strip search of an entire class is not contemplated by the "special need" doctrine and opens a Pandora's Box of claims of invasion of privacy against police or others involved.

Case 17
Thomas v. Roberts (11th Cir., 2001)

A fifth grader brought twenty-six dollars to school that he had raised selling candy for a school trip fund. The teacher had not arrived yet so he placed the envelope with cash on the teacher's desk and joined others watching a fight between two of his classmates. At some point the envelope with cash disappeared. When the teacher arrived, he reported the theft and the teacher queried the class about the missing envelope but got nowhere.

She knew there was police presence that day in school so she called the police officer to the classroom. He agreed with her suggestion that a search of the involved students was in order: she would do the girls and he would search the boys. Accordingly, the young males were taken off to the washroom where the officer demonstrated what he expected of them. He set his gun and holster aside and dropped his trousers to his knees. "You'll all do that," he said, "or I'll take you downtown in cuffs." There were no objectors.

In turn, each of the males dropped their trousers, and there was giggling at those who had misunderstood and dropped their underpants. No cash was found. Meanwhile, the teacher performed a similar search of the girls—but she conducted a much more extensive search, lifting each young lady's bra. In the end, the envelope and money were never found. But the search did have one financial result: shortly thereafter attorneys for the students involved filed suit against the school, police officer, and teacher, seeking damages for invasion of privacy.

At trial, the lower court held that the search had invaded the privacy of the children and found the school, officer, and teacher liable. The defendants appealed.

In a case with similar facts, on appeal to the federal 11th Circuit, the court affirmed the judgment. But, in a strange twist, the court released the defendants from liability for a reason none could have counted on. The court held that since no one before had ever been so stupid as to strip search an entire class, there was no way these defendants would have known in advance the search was illegal. School searches of children at the time were controlled by *New Jersey v. T.L.O.*, 469 U.S. 325 (1985). *T.L.O.* held student searches were based on individualized suspicion. The law to that date did not cover either strip searches or searches of an entire class. Accordingly, the court held the defendants warranted immunity.

Said the court:

> *We have little trouble in concluding, ... that the strip searches in this case were unconstitutional. As noted [in] T.L.O ... a school official must have "reasonable grounds" for suspecting that a student is guilty of a violation of school rules or the law. While declining to decide if individualized suspicion was a necessary element of the reasonableness standard in school searches, the [T.L.O.] Court noted that the requirement that officials possess suspicion that a particular student committed an illicit act before searching the student is subject to a very limited exception. (emphasis added)*
>
> *Given the circumstances of the money's disappearance, [the teacher] reasonably suspected that a student in her class had taken the envelope. However, [she and the officer] did not possess individualized suspicion that pointed to a specific student or group of students as responsible. In order to determine whether the searches were justified ... we must therefore first ask whether the searches were justified absent individualized suspicion.*
>
> *The Supreme Court has held that a search may be conducted without individualized suspicion when "the privacy interests implicated by the search are minimal, and ... an important governmental interest furthered by the intrusion would be placed in jeopardy by a requirement of individualized suspicion." [In a prior Supreme Court case. Skinner, the court had permitted random drug testing of athletes' urine on evidence of widespread drug use among student athletes.]*
>
> *Applying the Skinner balancing test to ... the searches conducted here, however, leads to a different result. Stu-*

dents in the school environment have lesser expectations of privacy than members of the general public. However, there is no question that schoolchildren retain a legitimate expectation of privacy in their persons, including an expectation that one should be able to avoid the unwanted exposure of one's body, especially one's "private parts." Although students may surrender some expectations of privacy when they enter the schoolhouse door, an expectation that they will be free from forced strip searches is not one of them. We therefore conclude that the students had an important privacy interest in not being unclothed involuntarily ... There has simply been no showing here that important government interests were in such jeopardy that an intrusive mass search was permissible. We therefore conclude that the alleged theft of twenty-six dollars, while certainly not insignificant in the context of a grade school, does not present such an extreme threat to school discipline or safety that children may be subject to intrusive strip searches without individualized suspicion. Because the strip searches in this case were conducted without individualized suspicion, they were not justified at their inception and were thus unreasonable under the Fourth Amendment.

Qualified Immunity

Qualified immunity provides complete protection for government officials sued in their individual capacities as long as "their conduct violates no 'clearly established statutory or constitutional rights of which a reasonable person would have known.' " In order for the law to be "clearly established," it must have been developed at the time of the alleged violation "in such a concrete and factually defined context to make it obvious to all reasonable government actors, in the defendant's place, that 'what he is doing' violates federal law." The pre-existing law must "truly compel (not just suggest or allow or raise a question about)" the conclusion that "what defendant is doing violates federal law in the circumstances." Law can be clearly established in this circuit only by decisions of the U.S. Supreme Court, this court, or the highest court of the state from which the case arose.

The district court concluded that [the teacher and officer] were entitled to qualified immunity because it was not clearly established at the time of the searches that strip searching the children en masse was unconstitutional.

It is ... difficult to imagine how school officials reading [prior cases] would have found themselves compelled to conclude that the searches in this case were constitutionally impermissible. Although a reasonable school official might have paused before strip searching a class of fifth graders, the best she could have discovered from a reading of the available case law was that a court may later determine that the searches were unreasonable. We conclude that the law was not developed in such a factually defined context that the individual defendants should have been aware that they were acting illegally when they either ordered or performed the searches in question. The district court therefore did not err in granting [the teacher and officer] qualified immunity.

Thomas v. Roberts, 261 F3d 1160 (11th Cr., 2001)

Chapter Ten
SCOPES AND THE NATURAL EYE, ETC.

In general, what the natural eye can see from a "place the viewer has a right to be" does not create a privacy issue. By natural eye we mean a view not enhanced by use of a scope. By scope we mean binoculars, telescopes, or hi-powered camera zoom lens. By a "place the viewer has a right to be" we mean a location in which others may complain of trespass, but the subject of the investigator's surveillance cannot. This might be a public sidewalk, a neighbor's property, or even the subject's walkway leading to the residence, or an open field behind the subject's home where others travel freely.

A home occupant may have every reasonable expectation that a post-it note grocery list stuck on the refrigerator door cannot be read by a passerby using his natural eyesight. While the passerby is in a place he has a right to be, the post-it is private. The occupant expects that it is private. The print is small. His expectation is reasonable. Now enters an investigator who wants to read what's on the note. Well, since the expectation of privacy in the note is reasonable, the investigator will need a warrant to see it. Okay, let's say that rather than a note, the occupant tapes a sign to the refrigerator. The occupant knows that the sign can be seen and read by someone in the public way. Can he make reasonable argument that his rights to privacy in the sign are protected? Well, he is mistaken if he thinks so. Where does the scope come in? Does it surprise you that the scope can be used to read the sign that can be read with the natural eye but cannot be used to read the post-it? Well, that is the irony of using scopes. They are okay when you don't need them to see; just neat to have to change positions for tactical reasons.

Said another way, a scoped view is not intrusive when the same view is attainable with the naked eye; but becomes intrusive when the view is not so attainable. By way of example, say an investigator moves to the edge of the subject's property to observe his query's activities. Let's dispose of one issue immediately. For this observation he is in a place he has a right to be. If there is a complaint of trespassing, it cannot be lodged by the subject. The view the investigator seeks is available to the neighbor, anytime he walks to the edge of his property. So any argument by the subject that he had a reasonable expectation of privacy when viewed from that location fails. To get on with our example: From his spot on the lot line the investigator observes through an open door the subject lifting weights in a barn behind his home. Let us assume lifting weights is an activity which would debase the subject's claim of total disability. If he can prove this disability he is a rich man. The investigator is paid a large sum of money to get this right. He uses his natural eyesight for this observation from a place he has a right to be but is in the open and can easily be seen by the subject. While there would be no privacy intrusion if he stayed at that locale, the jig would soon be up. The subject would spot him and drop the barbells to run in the house for his gun. Nothing ruins surveillance quicker than the spy being spied on.

So, not new to this business, the investigator abandons the lot line and moves back a hundred yards or more into some woods to stay out of sight of his subject. Of course, while the weight-lifter can't see him, neither can he see the weightlifter. A lesser man would go home. But our investigator has a plan. He comes equipped. He breaks out a camera with telephoto lens. Not some store bought kid's camera that gives a modest magnification. He has a professional camera bought for the occasion, one that will photograph sweat on the subject's pectorals the same as using a regular camera from the lot line. This camera will easily mimic the exact view the investigator had at the lot line without risk of discovery. He has not enhanced his view at all; he has merely moved it to a safer location. And now he has photographs to prove it!

Since the subject's activities are now observable from a location the investigator had a right to be, using a lens that does not enhance what he could have seen from the lot line, the weight lifter has no grounds to prove invasion of privacy. There was no privacy to intrude on. Okay, surely someone can complain of the trespass. Yes, the neighbor can. Of course our investigator should have asked for permission, but to do so, he knew he ran the risk that the neighbor and his subject were friends. He made a decision to go without such permission. And yes, if discovered, the owner of the adjoining property may well have taken serious issue with the investigator's presence. In fact, he might not only claim trespass, but the property owner himself may have alleged invasion of privacy had the investigator came upon him and the cleaning lady in a compromising position back of the house. But, that did not happen, and the investigator got his pictures of his subject lifting weights and there was no privacy intrusion. In hindsight, the subject should have shut the barn door.

Let us then consider two common scenarios in the operative's use of a scope. Each of these views presumes an observation that steers clear of protected space, such as government installations, hospital rooms, public washrooms, locker-room and the like. Common sense, backed by appropriate laws, caution that these spaces are off-limits to uninvited observation unless by warrant or other authority.

- *On Public Property* – The operative goes to the limit of property accessible to the public. The investigator may now back out and use a scope, not to enhance, but to duplicate the same view he acquired with the naked eye at the closer location.
- *On Private Property* – The operative goes to the limit of private property adjoining the subject's property. The investigator may now back out and use a scope, not to enhance, but to duplicate the same view he acquired with the naked eye at the closer location. Photographs taken from that locale will establish there was no intrusion. Precedent cases also support use of an open field for this purpose, even if part of the subject's property, particularly so when this parcel is regularly traversed by the public.

Following are precedent cases which demonstrate typical privacy and Fourth Amendment search issues involving use of scopes. Note that when it comes to privacy intrusion, there is little or no distinction in the cases between the warrantless actions of police in acquiring a scoped view, or that of the private investigator making the same view. In either case, if the view has been unduly enhanced by use of a scope, there are negative consequences. In the case of the government agent, inadmissibility of evidence procured is sure to follow; in the case of the private investigator, he has breached his subject's reasonable expectation of privacy and is liable for invasion of privacy.

Case 18
State v. Jones (Wash., 1982)

Late afternoon, a squad car sits at the far end of a large public park parking lot. Two officers in the squad are there in response to recent complaints of park user's rowdy behavior, public intoxication, and littering. From inside the squad, the officers observe a pickup truck parked on the other end of the parking lot. One of the truck doors is open and the officers observe the truck occupants drinking from cans. The officers are able to observe with their natural eyesight the men are drinking but not sure if it is alcohol. They know they could drive closer; or even approach on foot, but in these cases they would surely be discovered. Or they could use binoculars, from their current location, and make the same observation they could if they stood right outside the door of the truck. An officer, using the binoculars, verifies the truck occupants are drinking beer, and watches one of the men place a cylinder object to his nose, ostensibly inhaling cocaine. The officers immediately draw their weapons and approach the vehicle. There, they discover open beer cans and drug paraphernalia. Arrests are made.

At trial, the defendants moved to suppress the evidence; that the police observation by binoculars of the defendant's actions in the truck were prohibited by the Fourth Amendment of the U.S. Constitution. That is, use of binoculars intruded into their reasonable expectation of privacy. Therefore, the visual search and seizure of evidence was illegal. The prosecution countered that what the officer with binoculars was nothing more than what could have seen by any person walking past the truck in the public way. The defendant's expectation of privacy was therefore unreasonable. The defendant's were found guilty and appealed.

In a case with similar facts, on appeal to the Washington Court of Appeals, the court affirmed the convictions.

Said the court:

The sole issue is whether the observation of the activities in the car with the aid of binoculars was prohibited by the United States or State Constitutions? It was not. The use of binoculars to view what is otherwise visible violates neither the Fourth Amendment nor its counterpart [our state] constitution.

The rule is that: Fourth Amendment restrictions should not be imposed when the police have done no more than: (1) use binoculars to observe more clearly or carefully that which was in the open and thus subject to some scrutiny by the naked eye from the same location; or (2) use binoculars to view at a distance that which they could have lawfully observed from closer proximity but for their desire not to reveal the ongoing surveillance.

In performing their peace keeping duties, the officers had a right to be where they were and also the right to act on what they saw. Neither their observations nor their subsequent approach to defendants' car violated any reasonable expectation of privacy.
State v. Jones, 653 P2d 1369 (Wa 1982)

Case 19
State v. Louis (Or., 1983)

A woman phoned local police to complain that a neighbor had an annoying habit: almost every afternoon, he stood nude in his living room window and waved a cane at passersby on the public sidewalk. The complainant invited police to use her home to confirm the action. The complainant's home was nearly a block from the offender's place. Officers took a position in the complaint's living room but could not see the defendant in his front window from such a distance. The woman suggested they use binoculars, the same as had she. The officers had their own equipment and employed a 135-millimeter telephoto lens to get pictures of the man as he stood nude in his window waving a cane at persons on the public sidewalk. The defendant was charged with indecent exposure.

At trial, his attorney argued that his client had privacy protection in his home against those using a high-powered scope and camera to observe him. The prosecution countered that the defendant's expectation of privacy in his front window was unreasonable. Police could have taken a position in front of the defendant's house and seen the same view they acquired with the scope. It was a tactical option to keep their distance. The defendant was found guilty and appealed.

In a case with similar facts, on appeal to the Supreme Court of Oregon, the court affirmed the conviction.

Said the court:

It is generally understood that normal eyesight employed from a place the viewer has a right to be is a lawful view not requiring a search warrant: use of any scope or camera lens which enhances the normal view, even from a lawful place, may constitute a search and even invasion of privacy. In this case, the court admitted the photographs, saying: "The photographs [taken] as evidence in this case ... merely recorded what could be seen and had been seen without the camera (135mm lens)."
                    State v. Louis, 672 P2d 708 (Or 1983)

Chapter Ten 87

Case 20
People v. Arno (Cal., 1979)

Police received a tip of a pornographic film distribution operation occurring in the eighth-floor office of a local building. To observe activities within the office, officers set up operations on a hill level with and directly across from the office. The officers' location on the hill was separated from the building by a deep impassable gulley.

From their base, the officers could not discern activities in the office and could get no closer due to the gulley. A high-powered scope was brought in. Using the scope, officers could now observe eight-millimeter pornographic films stacked on a conference room table. Based on this observation, the officers procured a search warrant and raided the office. Arrests and prosecution followed.

The defendants filed a motion to suppress use of the scoped observation as an illegal search—the view with the scope invaded the reasonable expectation of privacy of the room's occupants. The defendants claimed that because of the impassable gulley, they had a right to presume what they did in the room was private. The gulley was no different than had there been a wall separating police from the room's activities. Accordingly, they argued, a search warrant was necessary for the scoped observation.

The trial court disagreed, and said the observation, which justified the warrant, was based on a plain-view observation of illegality. Had the men walked up to the window they could have seen the same sight as that provided by binoculars. The only reason they didn't go up to the window was because the gulley could not be traversed. Had the defendants been on the ground level, rather than the eighth floor, the officers could have walked right up to the window and gotten the same view as what they acquired with binoculars. The defendants were convicted and appealed.

In a case with similar facts, the California Court of Appeals reversed. The court held that the view enhanced by binoculars was an invasion of privacy. The court held that the expectation of privacy of the defendants was based on their confidence that what occurred inside the office was not visible to the naked eye from a place the officer or any third person had a right to be. Because of the gulley, there was no way, short of a helicopter, that the officers could come closer and they simply could not see inside the office with their naked eye sufficient detail to determine incriminating evidence was present. The view required a warrant.

Said the court:

We start then with Katz v. United States, [in which] the high court declared: "(T)he Fourth Amendment protects people, not places. What a person knowingly exposes to the public, even in his own home or office, is not a subject of Fourth Amendment protection. But what he seeks to preserve as private, even in an area accessible to the public, may be constitutionally protected."

...We thus view the test of validity of the surveillance as turning upon whether that which is perceived or heard is that which is conducted with a reasonable expectation of privacy and not upon the means used to view it or hear it. So long as that which is viewed or heard is perceptible to the naked eye or unaided ear, the person seen or heard has no reasonable expectation of privacy in what occurs. Because he has no reasonable expectation of privacy, governmental authority may use technological aids to visual or aural enhancement of whatever type available. However, the reasonable expectation of privacy extends to that which cannot be seen by the naked eye or heard by the unaided ear. While governmental authority may use a technological device to avoid detection of its own law enforcement activity, it may not use the same device to invade the protected right.

> *Here the activity seen through [the] ten-power binoculars within suite 804 was not observable to anyone not using an optical aid. It was as much protected from the uninvited eye as was Katz's conversation from the uninvited ear. We hence conclude that the municipal court erred in denying defendants' motion to suppress the product of [the] observations.*
>
> *People v. Arno,* 153 CalRptr 624 (Cal 1979)

Chapter Eleven
NON-ELECTRONIC EAVESDROP

Natural hearing, like natural eyesight, used from a place the observer has a right to be, renders what is heard a non-search, requiring neither warrant nor warrant exception.

As stated by the 9th Circuit Court of Appeals in the 1973 case of *U.S. v. Fisch:*

"Listening at the door to conversations in the next room is not a neighborly or nice thing to do. It is not genteel. But so conceding we do not forget that we are dealing here with the "competitive enterprise of ferreting out crime...[Using a room anyone could have rented, the officers] were under no duty to warn the appellants to speak softly, to put them on notice that the officers were both watching and listening."

Case 21
U.S. v. Mankani (2nd Cir, 1984)

The Drug Enforcement Agency (DEA) took occupancy of Room 113 of the Red Eye Motel. The agents acted on a tip that a meeting was about to occur involving the exportation of marijuana locally farmed. Conveniently, agents found a small hole in the wall between their room and that of the defendants. Using the hole in the wall, they were able to listen in to the meeting. Later, they would claim the hole must have been made by mice.

In any event, a sharp-eared DEA agent sat at the hole and listened. What he heard was a plan to flood the local community with enough cannabis to satisfy the appetite of every user within miles. The agent was impressed with the size of the operation, as was the judge who signed warrants of arrest. At trial, the defendants argued their expectation of privacy behind locked doors in a rented motel room was reasonable and that what police overheard constituted an illegal search. They were convicted and appealed.

In a case with similar facts, in affirming the convictions, the federal Second Circuit of Appeals said:

Whether overhearing this conversation constituted an unlawful search or seizure in violation of Fourth Amendment rights depends on whether these defendants under the circumstances had a reasonable expectation of privacy. If [the defendants] had a reasonable expectation of privacy in their conversation in the Sheraton Hotel room, then the warrantless "seizure" of that conversation violated the Fourth Amendment. If not, the district court, after conducting a hearing on this issue, properly denied their motion to suppress the conversation.

The [critical] factor is whether the agents had a legal right to be in the adjoining room and, if so, whether the defendants could reasonably have anticipated the agents' right to be there. In analyzing this factor the location of [the agent], with his ear pressed to the hole in the wall, must be carefully scrutinized. Just as what an officer sees when lawfully present is considered nonintrusive plain view, what he hears while so stationed is similarly not a search and seizure and is thus per se lawful.

Turning ... to the place where the eavesdropping took place, we acknowledge that the occupants of a hotel room are entitled to Fourth Amendment protection. A guest in a hotel room, like the occupant of a room in a boarding house or of an apartment or house, has the same constitutional rights against unreasonable searches and seizures. Thus, it is not the common hallway, entryway or passage alone that diminishes one's reasonable expectation of privacy in a hotel or motel room. Instead, it is the fact that hotels, as opposed to residences, are truly transitory places. Unlike an apartment or a room in a boarding house, hotels and motels are not ordinarily considered places where one lives and keeps personal effects. In addition, service personnel in hotels and motels have keys to enter and make-up the rooms, remove dishes, check air-conditioning, heating and the like. Former occupants may even have retained a key to a hotel room. Indeed, the presence of a visible door, crack or opening in a wall adjacent to another hotel room, as was the case here, should suggest to the average person that his or her privacy may be limited.

In short, it is the transitory nature of such places, commonly understood as such, that diminishes a person's justifiable expectation of privacy in them. Since a hotel room is exposed to others, it is unlike a "house," i.e., a place where one lives. Therefore, there is an accepted loss of privacy when one occupies a public place, somewhat akin to a conversation in the street, and the intervention of a human ear in those surroundings is the kind of intrusion one should anticipate. A number of courts, including our own, have concluded that the intrusion of a human ear in similar circumstances is not an unlawful "seizure" of a conversation in a hotel or motel room.

We conclude from the foregoing analysis that in order for the government to prove the constitutionality of its intrusion against an individual's claim of a violation of a reasonable expectation of privacy, it must demonstrate that: (1) the place where the intrusion occurred is one where the individual did not have a justified expectation of privacy; (2) the intrusion was not aided by mechanical or electronic means; and (3) the investigating officer was situated where an individual should anticipate that another person might have a right to be. Here defendants ... were in a Sheraton hotel room with a diminished expectation of privacy when their conversation was overheard by [the agent] listening with his ear pressed against an aperture from an adjoining room where the officer had a legal right to be. No physical, mechanical or electronic aids were used. Hence, the government has met its burden of justifying this intrusion and did not violate these defendants' Fourth Amendment rights.

U.S. v. Mankani, 738 F2d 538 (2nd Cir 1984)

Chapter Twelve
PRIVATE SPACE

12A: Privacy Stalls

Police searches based on a court-approved warrant or some standard exception to the requirement of a warrant may well intrude into the subject's expectation of privacy but do not violate the Fourth Amendment of the U.S. Constitution. Our concern here is investigator action without such authority when faced with an obvious effort by the subject to keep his actions private. The officer's decision that the subject miscalculated his expectation of privacy carries risk. If the officer is wrong, and there is reasonable expectation of privacy on the part of the subject, any evidence procured by the officer's actions is suppressed from use in any prosecution and there is risk of an action for invasion of privacy. To demonstrate how difficult the investigator's decision can be, in the following precedent case, there are two defendants involved in the same act, but only one is found to have had a reasonable expectation of privacy. (We must forewarn that while this oft-cited case is based on public records, it is extremely salacious.)

Case 22
Liebman v. State (Texas, 1983)

Officer Jay Adam and a partner were assigned surveillance duties in response to citizen complaints of rampant illegal sexual activity at a local adult video store. The store advertised itself as providing private booths for viewing of "fantasy" videos; i.e., pornographic videos. In plainclothes and requisite false mustache, the officers entered the store to observe activities of the patrons.

In time, Adam observed a subject, later identified as Bloomer, enter a private-booth labeled 14 and shut the door. Immediately thereafter, he observed another subject, later identified as Liebman, enter the adjacent booth 15 and shut his door. Now with Bloomer in booth 14, and Liebman in booth 15, and with both stall doors shut, the two subjects were separated only by a thin partition wall of plywood which Adam had already determined contained a pre-drilled hole waist high. The hole permitted easy "access" between the stalls. In police vernacular, this hole was known as the "glory hole," measuring just a few inches in diameter. The hole, not used for viewing movies, was well worn by use.

With both men in their respective booths, and doors to both booths closed, Adam and the other officer entered booth 13, to the left of booth 14. Adam closed his own booth door to ensure privacy from hallway passers-by. Next, silently so as not to disturb Bloomer and Liebman, Adam had his partner cup his hands so that Adam could step up and see over the seven-foot high partition wall into booth 14. Now with a clear view into booth 14, Adam saw Bloomer with his "body in the approximate location of the glory hole," standing "flushed against the wall with his hands out ... and his waist and entire body appeared to be flushed with the wall. That was the common wall that had the hole in it, facing booth number 15."

Satisfied they had half of the story, the officers moved to booth 16, to the right of 15, the booth occupied by Liebman. Again, door closed behind them, to "exclude intruding eyes," the officers repeated the sequence with Adam boosted up to the top of the partition. This time when he looked down, he "observed Liebman ... seated on a bench with his hands in skin contact with the (male organ) that was stuck through the wall from booth 14 into Booth 15 and he was (exercising) the (male organ) in a vigorous manner."

Since events were very hectic in and about the glory hole at that particular moment, Adam told his partner it was protocol to wait a few moments before they made the bust. When things settled down, the officers arrested both subjects. Prosecution for lewd behavior followed. At trial, the defendants argued their privacy had been invaded by an illegal police search; they claimed that when an individual goes into a private booth to observe pornographic movies and shuts the door behind him, he does not expect police to climb to the top of the adjoining seven-foot partition to observe his activities. Under such circumstances, the police observation constituted an illegal search and invasion of privacy.

The state countered that when an officer looks over a wall "only" seven feet high to look down into an adjoining booth, the officer is doing no more than any citizen could do if he chose to take the time and effort to do so. The view was there for any person with a ladder or another man's cupped hands. In effect, the peek over the partition walls from booth 13 into 14 and from 16 into 15 was open to anyone who cared to look—a non-search in a public place. There was no reasonable expectation of privacy. The trial court agreed and convicted both men.

In a case with similar facts, the Appeals Court of Texas analyzed the predicament of both subjects and came to a different conclusion for each. The court reversed the conviction of the occupant of booth 14, Bloomer. The court found that Bloomer had a reasonable expectation of privacy when he shut the door to his booth; that looking over the wall by police into Bloomer's stall was intrusive and not something that Bloomer should have anticipated; therefore, his conviction was overturned. But, as to Liebman, the court found that when the officer looked down into Bloomer's stall and saw him flush against the glory hole, he had probable cause to suspect a crime occurring on the other side of the wall; namely, that Liebman was performing a sex act on his side of the wall. Police then lawfully confirmed their suspicions by looking over the wall into Liebman's booth. Thus, the court reasoned there was probable cause and existence of a warrant exception to justify the arrest and conviction of Liebman. It was Liebman's bad luck the police looked into Bloomer's booth first.

Said the court:

We first observe that a finding that a place is "public," is not [the same as] concluding that one has no reasonable expectation of privacy in that place. Conversely, neither is it indispensable to concluding one has a reasonable expectation of privacy in a place, that the place is "nonpublic" or "private."

This verity was most succinctly acknowledged by the Supreme Court of the United States in Katz v. United States:

"What a person knowingly exposes to the public, even in his own home or office, is not a subject of Fourth Amendment protection. But what he seeks to preserve as private even in an area accessible to the public, may be constitutionally protected."

A determinative issue we confront is whether the officers' conduct in boosting one another to the only vantage points from which appellants could be observed constituted "searches" within the meaning of the Fourth Amendment to the Constitution of the United States. The State correctly observes that this issue depends on whether each appellant can claim a "reasonable" expectation of privacy which has been invaded, and which entitles him to the protection of the Fourth Amendment.

While the design of the "place" in which [Bloomer and Liebman/appellants] were observed by the officers is important, its relevance is in reflecting the inherent opportunity the individual had for privacy in the "place" and the steps he actually took to avail himself of that opportunity.

In this case, appellants entered booths constructed of plywood walls and a door, all of which were approximately seven feet high. The design of each of the 50 booths was such that, by placing a quarter in a slot, a movie would be projected onto the inside of the door where there was a projection screen. It was [the officer's] testimony that, with the door closed, no one could see "into the booths through a crack in the door." "Most of [the booths] do have locks." The tops of all the booths were open, and "anyone can look over the tops."

When appellants entered the booths in question, they "closed the door completely," even though, according to [the officer], it is not necessary to completely close the door in order to view the film. The officer testified that unless one were standing on something, or over seven feet tall, he could not see into other booths.

Accordingly, it is clear that a person would have a subjective expectation of privacy under the circumstances and conditions described. "A toilet stall in a public restroom is private to the extent it is offered to the public for private, however transient, individual use. The occupants are entitled to the modicum of privacy its design affords. Similarly, the 3½' x 4' booths in the Paris Theatre were offered to the public, including appellants, for private, however transient use. Appellants apparently took all steps possible to exclude others from the booths.

The second question in determining whether a "search" occurred requires an inquiry into whether appellants' subjective expectations of privacy were such that society is prepared to recognize them as "reasonable," or, stated another way, whether appellants' expectations, viewed objectively, were "justifiable" under the circumstances.

[T]he evidence adduced in the instant case indicates the management of the Paris Theatre expected their patrons to have privacy in the viewing booths. Thus, from all the facts and circumstances it is apparent that appellants' subjective expectations of privacy while in the booths, viewed objectively, were justifiable and those which society would be prepared to recognize as reasonable.

We are constrained to conclude in this case that the officers' conduct ... constituted "searches" within the meaning of the Fourth Amendment, and we so hold. [The court, however, affirmed poor Liebman's conviction on the basis that once police looked over Bloomer's wall, and saw him in contact with Bloomer through the hole in the wall they had evidence of probable cause; hence, based on the warrant exception of exigent circumstance, dissipation of

evidence unless action is taken immediately, the search of Liebman was legal and his arrest lawful.)
Liebman v. State of Texas, 652 SW2d 942 (Tex 1983)

Case 23
Green v. State (Tex., 1978)

Officer Able was assigned undercover duties at Mr. Peeper's Video Store in answer to complaints of public displays of indecent sexual behavior. He entered the video store and perused the magazines, none suitable for family reading, and watched. Adjoining the magazine rack and counter was a hallway with a row of booths. The booths came equipped with video machines where customers could play the pornographic videos rented at the counter. The booths were basically dark, lit only by multi-colored string lights that hung along the wall. In an effort to insure privacy for the patrons, the booths came equipped with full-length cloth curtains and a red light which was activated by counter personnel when the booth was in use.

Officer Able passed through the magazine section into the booth area to check things out. He could hear the melodious voice of a canned Johnny Mathias song piped through the hallway speakers and sensed romance in the air. Able took a seat at the far-end of the hall, from which he could observe the entrances to all booths. The hallway was quite busy with men in various trade and business dress entering many of the booths.

Able saw a bald man in work coveralls enter a booth numbered 18. The man was followed by another male subject in suit and tie who also entered booth number 18. The curtain was closed but the red light did not go on. Able walked to booth number 18 to look through a small gap in the curtain. He saw that a porno video movie was rolling but that the movie was not the only action. He watched the bald headed man "fondle the other man, unzip his pants, remove his (male organ) and (exercise same)." He then saw the man in the suit "put his head in (the other man's) crotch area." Then, "with his (male organ) still in the mouth of the man in the suit," the (man in coveralls) moved "his hips back and forth, and (there was) a loud sucking sound."

Officer Able threw the curtain aside and arrested both men for public indecency. At trial, the defendants argued that Officer Able's surreptitious look into the private booth was an illegal search—an intrusion into private space in which the subjects had reasonable expectation of privacy. They argued that when they closed the booth curtain, they indicated a expectation of privacy. The prosecution countered that what can be seen through curtain on a booth is a public view in which no one can claim an expectation of privacy. As further proof, the red light on the wall outside the booth was not on. Obviously, any member of the public could have moved the curtain unaware the booth was in use. Both men were convicted; but only the man in the suit appealed.

In a case with similar facts, the Court of Criminal Appeals of Texas affirmed the conviction holding that what Officer Able viewed was a public act. There was no privacy protection afforded by the loose curtain. As further evidence that the booth afforded no privacy protection, the light was not activated. The officer's action was in effect a non-search; and as such, the Fourth Amendment did not apply.

Said the court:

"What a person knowingly exposes to the public, even in his own home or office, is not subject to Fourth Amendment protection." Katz v. United States. A search means, of necessity, a quest for, a looking for, or a seeking out of that which offends against the law. This implies a prying into hidden places for that which is concealed. It is simply not a search to observe that which is open to view.

In Buchanan v. State, we were confronted with whether the defendant had a reasonable expectation of privacy in two different toilet stalls located in two different public restrooms. One of the restrooms was located inside a Sears store while the other was located in a public park. The toilet stall at the Sears store had doors which locked from the inside. The toilet stall in the public park had no doors and was visible to all in the general restroom area. Although police officers had viewed the defendant's illegal sex acts in both stalls from concealed positions above the toilet stalls, we held there that the defendant's expectation of privacy was not reasonable where no doors were provided for the stalls. There is quite a difference in one's expectation of privacy when he goes into a stall in a restroom with a door closed from the expectation of privacy in a peep show stall with the curtain open.

In the present case, [the officer] had a legal right to be in the hallway outside the booth. A three to five-inch gap between the curtain and the edge of the booth enabled the officers to view appellant's conduct. [The light over the stall was not lite. We hold there was no reasonable expectation of privacy.] We hold that [the officer's] conduct did not constitute a search.

Green v. State of Texas, 566 SW2d 578 (Tex 1978)

Case 24
People v. Mercado (NY, 1986)

Airport officials had received complaints of drug dealing in airport toilets. A police officer was assigned to watch the toilets and when alerted that two men had entered the same toilet stall, he hurried to the scene.

Airport toilet stalls had an eighteen-inch opening between the floor and bottom of the partition. When

Chapter Twelve

the officer entered the washroom he could hear two voices in one of the toilets but looking under the partition wall, he observed only one pair of legs. The officer dropped to the floor where he observed one subject sitting on the toilet closet with his feet on the seat and the other handing him a clear plastic bag with white powder. The officer jumped to his feet, pushed open the toilet door and arrested both men, seizing the powder before it could be flushed. The subjects were charged with illegal possession. At trial they argued their toilet stall became private space when they closed the door behind them. They were convicted.

In a case with similar facts, the Court of Appeals of New York affirmed the convictions, holding that the expectation of privacy in the toilet stall under these circumstances was not reasonable.

Said the court:

*The Fourth Amendment protects all citizens "from unreasonable government intrusions into * * * legitimate expectations of privacy" ... It does not protect every subjective expectation of privacy, but only those that society recognizes as reasonable. Once it is resolved that the particular locale is one in which there is a cognizable expectation of privacy, the invasion of that privacy interest—including a visual one—will be a search subject to constitutional strictures. Of course, since the Fourth Amendment protects against only unreasonable intrusions, [an immediate search under some circumstances] may be justified by the existence of probable cause to believe that a crime has occurred, is occurring or is about to take place.*

Persons have a reasonable expectation of privacy, for example, in their homes. The Supreme Court has also recognized a reasonable expectation of privacy in places that are nominally public ... [such as a telephone booth]. By the same token, an expectation of privacy in a public rest room toilet stall is reasonable. The enclosure exists precisely to insure privacy and to shield its occupant from public view ... Once the door is closed, an individual is entitled to assume that while inside he or she will not be viewed by others. The expectation of privacy, however, forecloses only unreasonable government intrusion.

Suspicion of criminal conduct does not negate one's privacy interest, but particular circumstances may give rise to cause for permissible intrusion [such as presence of probable cause and an exigent circumstance]. Here we conclude that the circumstances present gave [the officer] the requisite basis for looking into the stall.

[The officer] was working in airport security. While investigating a tip, without any illegal conduct, and through application of his experience and senses, he ascertained that two men were using a single toilet stall in a manner that indicated to him that the stall was not being used for its intended purpose. There was no evidence of a wheelchair, crutches or other device that might have suggested occupancy by a handicapped person in need of assistance, and the sight of only one pair of feet rendered it unlikely that one of the occupants was ill and being helped. [He] first pursued his investigation from afar, but based on what he could see and hear, he testified he suspected that the men were engaged in "a drug crime" or a "sex crime." Such activity within the stall could abruptly terminate, and evidence disappears, upon announcement of his presence.

Probable cause does not require proof to a mathematical certainty, or proof beyond a reasonable doubt. Based on the articulated, objective facts before [him], and the reasonable inferences to be drawn therefrom, it was "more probable than not" that criminal activity was taking place inside that stall. His suspicions heightened by what he saw and heard from afar, the officer was not compelled to turn heel and leave the rest room, but could properly look through the spaces at the sides of the door in an effort to learn what was going on inside. When those observations served only to enhance his suspicion of illicit activity, he properly entered the adjoining stall and looked over the partition. [Note: probable cause for search in this instance was based on an exigent circumstance: destruction of evidence unless the officer took immediate action.]

People v. Mercado, 501 NE2d 27 (NY 1986)

Chapter Twelve

12B: Changing Rooms

Can one successfully claim a reasonable expectation of privacy in a changing room occupied by numerous other persons, including strangers?

> **Case 25**
> ***Trujillo v. City of Ontario (Cal., 1996)***

Access to the police locker room of the ninth district was restricted to police officers of the district, visiting officers on temporary assignment, and maintenance personnel. This encompassed nearly a hundred persons. When a locker was broken into and police equipment taken, police supervisors had a dilemma. Was the thief one of their own?

A police detective assigned to investigate decided to bring in outside help in case a fellow officer was involved. He called a private investigator, Ace Cannon, to assist. Cannon's suggestion was that the broken locker be repaired, relocked, and that a video camera be placed in the ceiling right over the locker. He said, thieves always return to the scene.

The camera was installed but the thief did not return. In fact, in time the camera was taken down and the VHS tapes that resulted from the long-time surveillance were stored in a back room and forgotten. In time, the department was moved and officers were enlisted to assist in the move. They would move some boxes, paperwork, and the like. One of the boxes, it so happened, contained the tapes taken in the locker room. During a lull in the move, one of the officers became curious and opened the box. Believing the tapes might be discarded porno evidence from days past, albeit still good educational viewing, the officer popped a tape into a VHS player. Officers gathered around to see what lessons the tape might contain.

What he and others saw was themselves in various stages of undress. More videos were played and more of the same. A union rep was called, and, in time, a class action lawsuit was instituted on behalf of officers against the department for invasion of privacy.

The city defended that no one can reasonably expect privacy in a room in which so many other persons are present, including numerous officers and maintenance personnel. The lower court held that the tapes did constitute invasion of privacy; and the city appealed.

In a case with similar facts, a federal district court agreed that the video surveillance of a locker room was invasion of privacy.

Said the court:

Plaintiffs contend that they had a subjective expectation of privacy because by using a non-public locker room for private conduct—showering, changing clothes, and using the toilets and urinals—they demonstrated their desire to perform these activities privately. Defendants assert that Plaintiffs have failed to present evidence that they took actions to preserve their privacy from other people while in the communal locker room.

One has a subjective expectation of privacy if one has taken efforts to preserve something as private. Here, Plaintiffs have presented sufficient evidence that they performed activities such as changing clothes and showering in the locker room and had a subjective expectation of privacy to be free from covert video surveillance. That Plaintiffs chose to perform these activities in an area specifically designed to protect their privacy instead of a public area establishes that they had taken measures to preserve these activities as private.

Defendants argue that Plaintiffs failed to take actions to protect their private activities because they "freely changed clothes" in the presence of others, but that fact is immaterial. First, Plaintiffs took measures that significantly limited the number of people who could observe their private activities. Second, Defendants' argument defies logic: A person can have a subjective expectation of privacy that he or she will not be covertly recorded, even though he or she knows there are other people in the locker room; just as a person can have a subjective expectation that his or her home will not be searched by the authorities, even if he or she has invited friends into his or her home. Third, as will be discussed below, Plaintiffs are not asserting that they had a subjective privacy expectation from the other officers present in the locker room; rather, they subjectively expected that they were free from covert video surveillance.

Thus, Plaintiffs' use of a locker room to change clothes is sufficient to establish that no reasonable jury could find that they did not take measures to preserve their actions as private. Here, Plaintiffs used the locker room to perform private activities such as changing clothes and showering and, indeed, the camera recorded Plaintiffs in various states of undress. Plaintiffs aptly concede that minimal intrusions are likely to occur and that they have no reasonable expectation of privacy from those intrusions. This does not diminish the reasonableness of a person's expectation to be free from covert video surveillance...Plaintiffs need not have an expectation of total privacy in order to have a reasonable expectation that they will not be recorded surreptitiously while changing clothes in a locker room. ("Privacy does not require solitude ... [A]ccess of others does not defeat [people's] expectation of privacy."); ("Even if one cannot expect total privacy while alone in another person's hotel room (i.e., a maid might enter, someone might peek through a window, or the host might reenter unannounced), this diminished privacy interest does not eliminate society's expectation to be protected from the severe intrusion of having the government monitor private activities through hidden video cameras.").
Trujillo v. City of Ontario, 428 FSupp2d 1094 (CD Cal 2006)

An expectation of privacy may be reasonable in a changing room frequented by others of the same sex, as the case-precedent above shows, but can there be a reasonable expectation of privacy in a room which is under video surveillance by others of the opposite sex?

Case 26
Bevans v. Smartt (D. Utah, 2004)

Police Officer Jenny Sharp and a fellow officer drew strip-club duty. Their assignment was to check the Heavy Bush Dance Club for code compliance. Specifically, they were to stop by and verify all dancers had proper city licenses.

When Officer Sharp and her male partner entered the club she noticed a dancer who avoided eye contact and immediately headed for the changing room. This was enough for Sharp to be suspicious and she followed the dancer to the changing room. On the door of the changing room was posted a sign which read: "Absolutely no admittance without authority. Room is Videoed."

Sharp, suspecting the dancer was unlicensed, called out for the woman to stop. But the dancer, later identified as Suzy G., ignored the call and slammed the changing room door behind her. Officer Sharp and her partner did not hesitate. They followed behind the dancer into the changing room and found themselves surrounded by several apparently outraged women in various stages of undress. Sharp cornered Suzy G. and demanded her license. A shouting match ensued and an uncooperative Suzy G. was arrested and charged with obstruction of justice.

At trial, Suzy G. was well defended and the court returned a verdict of not guilty; whereupon, her attorney immediately filed suit against the city and police department for invasion of Suzy G's privacy. The suit alleged intrusion into her reasonable expectation of privacy when the officers came into her changing room. At trial, the city argued that Suzy G. could not have a reasonable expectation of privacy in a room that had cameras beaming real-time video to management, including male supervisors and owners, in the front office. The trial court sustained the city motion for summary judgment and dismissed the case.

In a case with similar facts, on appeal to the 2d federal district court of Utah, the court reversed holding Suzy G. did have a reasonable expectation of privacy in the room notwithstanding the room was under video surveillance.

Said the court:

That expectation of privacy which is significant for the purposes of Fourth Amendment analysis has subjective and objective aspects. In order for a particular search to come within the Fourth Amendment's prohibition on unreasonable searches and seizures, a claimant must manifest a subjective expectation of privacy in the area searched, and that expectation must be one society is prepared to recognize as objectively reasonable.
Defendants maintain that Plaintiff could not manifest a subjective expectation of privacy in the dressing room because the room was under constant video surveillance, and because the room was sometimes entered by persons other than dancers and used for purposes other than changing clothes. Plaintiff's deposition testimony demonstrates, according to Defendants, that
[s]he knew she was under the watchful eye of a security camera that recorded her every move. She admits that the club's managers, dancers, disc jockeys, bartenders, hired photographers, and sometimes even patrons would enter the dressing room. She admits that other dancers would use the dressing rooms as a marketplace to sell clothing. These undisputed facts show that [the plaintiff] should have expected any number of people to walk into the dressing room without knocking while she was sitting there.

The fact that other dancers used the room is insignificant; the suggestion that patrons entered the dressing room is inaccurate. That other dancers used a dancers' dressing room hardly undermines a particular dancer's expectation of privacy in the room. The single reference in Plaintiff's Deposition to a patron attempting to enter the dressing room tends to reinforce rather than diminish Plaintiff's expectation of privacy, since the patron's efforts met with spirited resistance and were ultimately rebuffed. While Plaintiff does refer to disc jockeys and managerial staff entering the room, Defendants have not cited to any evidence in Plaintiff's Deposition indicating that those entries took place under normal conditions; managers or disc jockeys entered the dressing room only if a dancer was "late to stage" or in some sort of danger. The bartenders who entered the room appear from Plaintiff's deposition testimony to have been women, who used the room to change into the "extravagant clothing" no doubt suitable for tending bar at American Bush. Plaintiff's testimony also makes reference to photo shoots connected with the web site operated by the President and Chief Executive Officer of American Bush. While these photo shoots appear to be less connected to the regular business of American Bush than the other activities cited by Defendants, discrete, permissive, and anomalous entries by photographers are insufficient to defeat the dancers' reasonable expectation of privacy in the dressing room. The fact that dancers sometimes sold clothing in the dressing room is also insufficient to defeat the dancers' expectation of privacy, particularly since Defendants have offered no case law in support of the proposition that there can be no reasonable expectation of privacy in an area used for multiple purposes, only some of which are ordinarily considered to be private. In any event, Plaintiff's deposition testimony is clear on the point that the "majority" of the activities carried on in the dressing room consists of dancers changing clothes, which supports a finding that the Plaintiff had a subjective expectation of privacy in the dressing room.

Against these facts from Plaintiff's Deposition, Defendants set the presence of the video camera, which looms large in Defendants' arguments concerning the want of a reasonable expectation of privacy in the dressing room. Video camera surveillance appears, in Defendants' formulation, to undermine the subsistence of both a subjective and objective expectation of privacy. According to Defendants, Plaintiff's knowledge of the video camera is relevant to her subjective expectation of privacy: because Plaintiff was aware of the camera and implicitly consented to its presence when she failed to obstruct the video camera lens, "neither she nor the persons in the room present with her would have reasonable expectations of privacy." Defendants cite in support of this proposition case law ... holding that when an informant consents to video surveillance, someone with the informant in a hotel room has no reasonable expectation of privacy. These cases address the expectations of persons other than those who have consented to the surveillance, and whose criminal activities are being recorded by the police, and are not particularly apposite to the case before this Court.

That defendants in a criminal case may not assert a reasonable expectation of privacy when their interactions with informants are taped for law-enforcement purposes does not answer the question of whether an employee in a dressing room may still assert a reasonable expectation of privacy from police intrusion in a room taped by her employers in order to ensure her safety. The affidavit of the Club's President and Chief Executive Officer indicates the surveillance of the dressing room is motivated by a desire to protect the dancers: "the premises are monitored by security cameras for the safety of [the] employees only. Tapes are kept for only 24 hours, and then destroyed unless the safety of employees is in question." Plaintiff's subjective understanding accords with that of the Club's management: the purpose of the camera in the dressing room was "security also, safety."

Because the videotaping by the Club's management in the case before this Court was motivated by very different concerns than those which animated the law enforcement officers in the cases cited by Defendants, the Court must, in order to accept Defendants' arguments that the fact of videotaping is sufficient to destroy the reasonable *expectation of privacy, disregard the reasons for which videotaping is undertaken and by whom. In their discussion of qualified immunity, Defendants cite additional case law they suggest supports the proposition that there can be no reasonable expectation of privacy in an area subject to video surveillance. [This case law] might be persuasive authority if the case before this Court involved an assertion by Plaintiff that the decision by American Bush to place a video camera in the dressing room violated some reasonable expectation of privacy she enjoyed in the room. [These cases do not offer] this Court significant guidance in answering the question of whether the fact that an employer videotapes a workplace area for safety purposes destroys an employee's reasonable expectation of privacy for all other purposes, including warrantless intrusions by the police. [These cases rely] on the relatively public nature of the locations videotaped in justifying their rulings that employees in those locations did not enjoy a reasonable expectation of privacy. In the case before this Court, in contrast, the room in question is a private area, from which the public is excluded.*

Even if the room is not rendered a public space as a result of its use by a variety of people for a variety of purposes, Defendants appear to suggest that the videotaping, without more, transforms the room into a place in which no reasonable expectation of privacy is possible. The videotaping of the room for safety purposes does not by itself, however, eliminate the possibility that a reasonable expectation of privacy exists for some other purposes. Images of the dressing room are transmitted from the dressing room to only two monitors, one located at the disc jockey's booth and the other in the manager's office. There is no evidence to contradict the statement of the president and Chief Executive Officer of American Bush that the recording is only visible at a "small monitor at the DJ booth, where it is blocked off from the view of others" and in his office, where access "is limited to himself and other management personnel as necessary." Defendants argue that since "anyone with access to the images recorded by those cameras could see [Plaintiff] at any time," Plaintiff could have no reasonable expectation of privacy in the dressing room. While it is true that Plaintiff could have no reasonable expectation of privacy in the dressing room if the content of that expectation were that she would not be visible to the disc jockey or a manager, Defendants have neither offered argument nor cited any case law supporting the proposition that the fact that a person's activities were visible leads to the conclusion that that person has no expectation of privacy from police intrusions. If Plaintiff were to change clothes in her home without drawing the blinds, it seems unlikely that she would by that fact alone have relinquished any reasonable expectation of privacy in her home so that warrantless police searches would become permissible.

The legal authority on which Defendants rely does not ultimately support their position that there was no subjectively or objectively reasonable expectation of privacy in the dressing room. Indeed, the opposite conclusion, that there was a reasonable expectation of privacy in the dressing room, finds support in the very ordinance on which Defendants rely to justify warrantless administrative searches of sexually-oriented businesses. The Ordinance authorizes searches of those areas in a sexually-oriented business in which patrons are permitted, thereby creating an expectation that other areas of a sexually-oriented business will be free from warrantless searches made pursuant to the Ordinance. One of the requirements a legislative scheme authorizing warrantless administrative searches must fulfill in order to pass constitutional muster is that it provide the owner of the premises with the same certainty as a warrant: the statute must define the scope of the search and limit the discretion of the officers performing the search. It is reasonable to infer that if the statute itself puts owners (and their employees) on notice that certain areas of a business are subject to warrantless searches, then the statute simultaneously creates a reasonable expectation that other areas will not be exposed to police intrusion.

For the foregoing reasons, ... the police] motion for Summary Judgment ... is accordingly DENIED.

Bevans v. Smartt, 316 F.Supp.2d 1153 (D. Utah, 2004)

Chapter Thirteen
ABANDONED PROPERTY

An individual may claim ownership in property, say, his briefcase or other closed container, even after he sets the case down in a public area and walks away; but can he then claim privacy in the contents?

Case 27
U.S. v. Hernandez (10th Cir., 1993)

At the Border Patrol inspection area, Officer Dodger boarded a bus for a routine crossing inspection, looking for illegal immigrants and contraband. He eyeballed the half-full bus looking for "someone who stood out"; then opened the luggage compartment for perusal of passengers' luggage and other goods. When he looked back at the passengers, he glanced around to see who might be avoiding eye contact.

Dodger spotted a stout Hispanic, later identified as Hector Hernandez, with a wide-brimmed straw hat and open shirt who acted like he was looking out the window, but Dodger saw the man glance back at him out of the corner of his eye. Dodger feigned disinterest, and walked down the line looking at luggage. He spotted a solitary backpack in the overhead bin. Dodger knew Hispanics crossing the border never left their luggage less than an arm's reach away, so the bag was fair game.

He turned to Hernandez and asked in English, "This bag yours?"

Hernandez muttered back in Spanish, "I've got no luggage."

Dodger again announced in Spanish to the entire bus: "Who belongs to this bag?" No one answered. The bag was now his, and Dodger squeezed the bag hard. He felt the distinct outline of small packets. Soon he had a scent dog chewing open the backpack, spilling bundles of white powder onto the floor. The powder tested positive for cocaine.

It was now time for Dodger to make another announcement to passengers of the bus: "This bus is going nowhere until I find out who brought that backpack aboard." There was silence but for only a minute. Then, a female passenger stood up, pointed a finger at Herndandez, and said, "It's his. Let's get going." Hernandez was arrested and tried on drug charges.

At trial, counsel for the defendant argued that the border agent needed a search warrant to open a backpack. He said, "Absent a warrant or an appropriate warrant exception, a container such as a knapsack cannot be opened." The prosecution countered that what he said was true, but there existed an exception to the requirement of a warrant and that exception was present here: abandonment. He said there can be no reasonable expectation of privacy in an item that has been abandoned. When Hernandez disavowed ownership of the bag, he could not complain of its inspection. Hernandez was convicted and appealed.

In a case with similar facts, on appeal, the defendant's conviction was affirmed.

Said the 10th Circuit Court of Appeals:

A warrantless search and seizure of abandoned property is not unreasonable under the Fourth Amendment. Thus, if Agents ... accurately determined, through their routine checkpoint questions, that the backpack was abandoned, the agents' search did not violate the Fourth Amendment ...

The test for abandonment is whether an individual has retained any reasonable expectation of privacy in the object. This determination is made by objective standards. An expectation of privacy is a question of intent which may be inferred from words, acts, and other objective facts. The abandonment must be voluntary. For example, an abandonment is not voluntary when it results from a Fourth Amendment violation. However, police pursuit or investigation at the time of abandonment of property, without more, does not of itself render abandonment involuntary.

We conclude that the district court's determination that Defendant had abandoned his backpack was not clearly erroneous. Defendant elected to distance himself from the backpack upon boarding the bus and repeatedly failed to acknowledge ownership of the backpack after [the officer] repeatedly questioned the bus passengers regarding the backpack's ownership...Thus, we affirm the district court's determination that Defendant lacked standing to complain of a Fourth Amendment violation because he voluntarily abandoned the backpack.

U.S. v. Hernandez, 7 F3d 944 (10th Cir 1993)

Chapter Fourteen
TRASH

The curtilage of a home is generally defined as an area around the residence that is close enough for family activities. As such, it receives privacy protection to the extent that the expectation of privacy is reasonable. Thick bushes around the back-yard pool are an example. They are planted for privacy; and may make an effort to peep past them actionable as invasion of privacy. The front driveway of a private residence also is curtilage. Our question here is whether it is reasonable for the occupant to expect privacy protection for trash left in the driveway for city pickup.

Case 28
U.S. v. Hendricks (7th Cir., 1991)

DEA agent Browning was assigned a "trash pull" at the home of suspected drug dealer Tony Smith. A trash pull is an inspection of discarded garbage and may involve handling anything and everything from food to dog liter to drug needles. It is unpleasant, dirty business.

Browning did the pull regularly, inventorying the contents of a closed metal container placed weekly on Smith's driveway about fifty feet from the house and near an unattached garage. Browning usually performed his pull the night before scheduled city pickup. He worked only after dark, and was careful to shield himself from the home by working behind trees and bushes. He ultimately reached a point where enough evidence had been recovered that he could charge Smith as a drug dealer.

At trial, Smith moved to suppress the evidence recovered from his trash as fruit of an illegal search. He claimed his trash can was purposely left in his home's private curtilage so he could retain a reasonable expectation of privacy in the trash until pickup. He said entry into his curtilage to remove his trash was like entering his house for evidence. As such, a warrant or warrant exception was required. He was found guilty and appealed.

In a case with similar facts, on appeal to the United States Court of Appeals, Seventh Circuit, the defendant's conviction was affirmed.

Said the court:

> In *California v. Greenwood,* the [U.S.] Supreme Court held that the Fourth Amendment does not prohibit the warrantless search and seizure of garbage left for collection outside the curtilage of the home. At common law, the curtilage is the area encompassing the intimate activity associated with the sanctity of the home and the privacies of life. As a result, "[t]he protection afforded the curtilage is essentially a protection of families and personal privacy in an area intimately linked to the home, both physically and psychologically, where privacy expectations are most heightened." The Supreme Court has declared in numerous cases that the boundary of the curtilage is clearly marked for most homes as the area around the home to which the activity of home life extends. Those cases have recognized that the yard of a residential home is within the curtilage of the house. Therefore, the garbage cans located 20 feet from the garage and approximately 50 feet from the back door of the house were technically within the curtilage of the home, in which privacy expectations are most heightened.
> The mere intonation of curtilage, however, does not end the inquiry. The Supreme Court declared in *Katz v. United States,* that "[w]hat a person knowingly exposes to the public, even in his home or office, is not a subject of Fourth Amendment protection"; hence, views by police of enclosed backyards from airplanes do not violate the Fourth Amendment because the yard is readily visible to anyone glancing down from an airplane. The visibility of the yard

to the public and the routine nature of air flights renders the expectation of privacy unreasonable. Similarly, containers or sheds within the curtilage would not be protected if their contents could be viewed by people routinely passing on the street or overhead.

The Court has never indicated, however, that a container such as a backpack which was placed at the side of a driveway within the curtilage of a house could be searched without a warrant; in fact, case law indicates that such a container could not be searched because its contents are not in plain view and have not been knowingly exposed to the public. We must now determine, however, whether that container may be searched if it is a garbage can. The result can differ only if there is something in the nature of a garbage can which results in the exposure of its contents to the public.

The obvious distinction between garbage cans and other containers is that it is "common knowledge" that members of the public often sort through other people's garbage, and that the garbage is eventually removed by garbage collectors on a regular basis. Therefore, in order to extend Greenwood to this situation, we must determine that the garbage at this location was still readily accessible to the public, or that the intent eventually to convey the garbage to the garbage collector is itself sufficient to eliminate any expectation of privacy in garbage ... Therefore, the proper focus under Greenwood is whether the garbage was readily accessible to the public so as to render any expectation of privacy objectively unreasonable.

In other words, garbage placed where it is not only accessible to the public but likely to be viewed by the public is "knowingly exposed" to the public for Fourth Amendment purposes ... If the garbage is placed at the curb, the public has ready access to it from the street, and in fact can be expected to utilize that ability. On the other hand, garbage cans placed next to the house or the garage are not so accessible to the public that any privacy expectations are objectively unreasonable ...

The garbage cans in this case were permanently located at the side of the driveway, somewhat closer to the public sidewalk than the garage. In order to view the contents of the cans, "children, snoops, scavengers or other members of the public" would have to walk 18–20 feet from the sidewalk. Apparently, at least part of the driveway was visible from the house, because the officers that removed the garbage hid behind bushes and trees in approaching the cans. The cans themselves, however, could not be seen from the house because trees and bushes blocked the view from the back of the house.

Therefore, applying the Greenwood analysis to garbage within the curtilage, the relevant inquiry is whether the garbage cans were so readily accessible to the public that they exposed the contents to the public for Fourth Amendment purposes. Because the distance between the garbage cans and the public sidewalk was relatively short, the garbage was collected by the garbage service from that location, and the garbage cans were clearly visible from the sidewalk, we hold that Hendrick possessed no reasonable expectation of privacy in the garbage. As a general rule, the reasonableness of the expectation will increase as the garbage gets closer to the garage or house. In this case, the garbage was right in the middle of the driveway, and the proximity of the garbage cans to the sidewalk and the absence of a fence or any other barrier indicates that the garbage was knowingly exposed to the public. Accordingly, the decision of the district court denying the motion to suppress, and the conviction, is AFFIRMED.

U.S. v. Hendrick, 922 F2d 396 (7th Cir 1991)

Table of Cases

1. *Forster v. Manchester*, 189 A2d 147 (Pa 1963)
2. *Souder v. Pendleton*, 88 So2d 716 (La 1956)
3. *Nastal v. Henderson*, N0125069 (Mi 2006)
4. *Furman v. Sheppard*, 744 A2d 583 (Md 1998)
5. *Burns v. Masterbrand Cabinets*, 824 NE2d 72 (Ill 2007)
6. *Nobel v. Sears*, 109 CalRptr 269 (Cal 1973)
7. *McCain v. Boise Cascade*, 533 P2d 343 (Or 1975)
8. *Miller v. Brooks*, 472 SE 2d 350 (NC 1996)
9. *Keyzer v. Amerlink*, 618 SE2d 768 (NC 2005)
10. *Phillips v. Grendahl*, 312 F2d 357 (8th Cir 2002)
11. *Remsburg v. Docusearch*, 816 A2d 1001 (NH 2003)
12. *Johnson v. Kmart*, 723 NE2d 1192 (Ill 2002)
13. *Association Services v. Smith*, 549 SE2d 454 (Ga 2001)
14. *Gillette v. State of Texas*, 588 SW2d 361 (Tx 1979)
15. *State v. Buswell*, 449 NW2d 471 (Minn 1990)
16. *Hidey v. Ohio State Highway Patrol*, 689 NE2d 89 (Oh 1996)
17. *Thomas v. Roberts*, 261 F3d 1160 (11th Cir 2001)
18. *State v. Jones*, 653 P2d 1369 (Wa 1982)
19. *State v. Louis*, 672 P2d 708 (Or 1983)
20. *People v. Arno*, 153 CalRptr 624 (Cal 1979)
21. *U.S. v. Mankani*, 738 F2d 538 (2d Cir 1984)
22. *Liebman v. State of Texas*, 652 SW2d 942 (Tx 1983)
23. *Green v. State of Texas*, 566 SW2d 578 (Tx 1978)
24. *People v. Mercado*, 501 NE2d 27 (NY 1986)
25. *Trujillo v. City of Ontario*, 428 FSupp2d 1094 (CDCal 2004)
26. *Bevans v. Smartt*, 316 FSupp2d 1153 (DUtah, 2004)
27. *U.S. v. Hernandez*, 7F3d 944 (10th Cir 1993)
28. *U.S. v. Hendricks*, 922 F2d 396 (7th Cir 1991)

Notes

NOTES

OTHER TITLES OF INTEREST FROM LOOSELEAF LAW PUBLICATIONS, INC.

Navigating the Legal Minefields of Private Investigations
A Career-Saving Guide for Private Investigators, Detectives & Security Police
by Ron Hankin

Detecting Deception
The Science of Communication
by Inv. Paul S. McCormick

Real World Search & Seizure – *2nd Edition*
by Matthew J. Medina

Criminal Investigative Function - *2nd Edition*
A Guide for New Investigators
by Joseph L. Giacalone

Path of the Hunter
Entering and Excelling in the Field of Criminal Investigation
by Larry F. Jetmore, Ph.D., Capt., Hartford, CT PD (Ret.)

Handgun Combative – *2nd Edition*
by Dave Spaulding

Processing Under Pressure
Stress, Memory and Decision-Making in Law Enforcement
by Matthew J. Sharps

(800) 647-5547   www.LooseleafLaw.com

Index

Appropriation 3
Association Services, Inc. v. Smith 57
Bad ruse 26
Bevans v. Smartt 108
Buchanan v. State 102
Burns v. Masterbrand Cabinets 26
California v. Greenwood 120
Changing rooms 105
Credit information 40
Curtilage 119, 122
Drug Enforcement Agency (DEA) 91
Eavesdrop 91
Fair Credit Reporting Act (FCRA) 40, 43
False light 2
Federal Civil Rights Act, The 63
Finder's report 41, 43
Forster v. Manchester 5
Fourth Amendment 61, 65, 75, 88, 95, 103, 120
Furman v. Sheppard 23
Gillett v. Texas 65
Gontarez v. Smitty's Super Value 65
Good ruse 22
Green v. State 100
Hidey v. Ohio State Highway Patrol 71
Intrusion upon seclusion 55
Intrusive surveillance 11
Invasion of privacy 53, 57, 63
Invasion of privacy; four branches of 1
Invasive trespass 34
Johnson v. K-mart 53
Joye v. Hunterdon Cent. High School 75
Katz v. United States 61, 88, 101
Keyzer v. Amerlink 37
Lawful purpose 18
Liebman v. State 95
McCain v. Boise Cascade 31
Miller v. Brooks 34
Nastal v. Henderson 18
New Jersey v. T.L.O 77
Noble vs. Sears 28
People v. Arno 87

People v. Mercado 102
Phillips v. Grendahl 41
Police involvement 69
Private facts, public disclosure of 2
Private security 65
Private stalls 95
Prosser, William L. 1
Public eye 31
Public policing function 69
Publication of private facts 55
Qualified immunity 78
Reasonable expectation of privacy 61
Reasonable private policing 69
Reasonable suspicion 65
Remsburg v. Docusearch 45, 49
Restatement of Law 72
Rules of safe surveillance 13
Ruse 21
    bad 26
    good 22
Sale of unpublished information 45
School searches 75
Solitude and seclusion; intrusion of 1
Souder v. Pendleton 14
Stalking 17
State v. Buswell 67
State v. Louis 85
Thomas v. Roberts 75
Tort 1
    intrusion 44
    publication of private facts 44
Tort remedies 1
Trade line information 43
Trash pull 119
Trespass 30
Trujillo v. City of Ontario 105
U.S. v. Fisch 91
U.S. v. Hendricks 119
U.S. v. Hernandez 115
U.S. v. Mankini 91
United States in Katz v. United States 98
Warrant, exceptions, and non-search 62
Watch communities 12